A Sweet, Little Dream

Also by Morgan Straughan Comnick

Spirit Vision

A Sweet, Little Dream

Amai chisana yume
A short story collection

By Morgan Straughan Comnick

*This collection is dedicated to my Grandma Shirley Hutchings
and Mr. Tim Banger*

*Grandma, you are my sunshine, my inspiration to laugh, smile, and live life
to the fullest. Thank you for caring for me when I was sick, being my playmate,
my cartoon recorder (go, go Power Rangers!), my after school teacher, the person I
would run to when I needed warmth and love, and one of my best friends. You
were the first person to love me like a child and treat me like an adult. I know I
can talk to you about anything and you will never judge me and never stop loving
me for who I am. Because of you, I see that there is good in everyone and
everything and life is a beautiful gift. I love you with all my heart Grandma;
you're my* favorite!

*Mr. Banger, my freshman communication arts teacher, my father's co-
teacher, the role model for today's youth that has made his mark on our high
school forever. Thank you for pushing me so hard, allowing me to see I had
unpolished talent and make me care about my grammar and spelling, and for
your passion for writing and language and instilling it in me. I thrived off your
charismatic nature, your "sermons," your catch phrases (Jedi of Communication
Arts), and your eagerness for life. You will always be my publishing inspiration
and a true role model for today's youth and father figure to this young girl.*

Table of Contents

My Little Box (1997) 5

Your Eyes (2002) 7

The Warmth of Colors (2004) 11

My Love (2004) 13

Dearest Angel (2004) 17

Mystery (2004) 21

Time to Shine! (2004) 23

Sister (2005) 25

Prove My Heart Can Shine (2005) 27

Watch and See (2005) 31

Who is a Hero? (2006) 35

A Child's Rainy Day (2005) 37

My Favorite Signs (A Christmas Poem) (2005) 39

I See Now (2005) 41

Symbol of our Love (early 2006) 43

Frozen Still (2006) 45

Love is not the Word (2006) 47

Girls Know Nothing (spring 2006) 49

The Graduate I'm Proud Of (May 2006) 51

Even I Can . . . (2006) 55

Willing to Try (2006) 57

I Want to be Beautiful (2006) 61

All I can do is Observe You (2006) 63

Blinded 65

Now That You're Gone (2006) 67

He Slipped Away (2006) 71

Invisible Graduate (2007).. 73

I Will Never go any Further (2007) 77

Boys are Idiots (2007).. 79

Painful Game (2007) 83

Lonely Heart (2007) 85

Nature's Lesson (2007) 87

Stress (2007) 89

A Reason (2007) 91

Current Feelings (2007) 93

Don't Cry When I am Gone... 95

I Don't Understand.. 97

Tale of Roses and Bloom (1999)...................................... 101

Which are Better Pets? Cats or Dogs? (2004) 107

Reasons why Izzy Should or Shouldn't get a Part-time Job
(2004)... 113

1920s Skirt (2004) 119

Margaret's America 125

The Choice of Faith 133

The Cure for Sorrow.. 139

Wishing on a Star.. 147

How it all Started.. 153

Sleeping Earth... 163

Arctic Fun... 165

A Bird's Eye View 167

Smile 169

Between Worlds... 171

Visions... 173

My Comfort Zone 175

Ellis Island Journal Project 177

Medieval Journal of a Serf (2000) 183

When the Stars Lead the Way 189

"Hold me like I were a raindrop; tight enough so I cannot slip through your fingers, but not hard enough so I disappear into thin air."

—Morgan Straughan Comnick

Introduction

Ever since I learned what a collection was, I knew I wanted to share one! Before I tackled the writing a whole book challenge, I wrote short stories, plays, poems, poems, and . . . wait for it . . . more poems! Being a lover of music made writing "songs" an addiction for me, an amazing way to express myself when speaking failed me and since I was shy and awkward, spoken words failed me a lot. My over-active imagination and play times made writing scripts for actors and short stories a pleasure too. If the main characters in any of the writings sound familiar, I apologize. Even though I was a shy child, I was still a child and, as I later learned in college, children are *egocentric* by nature.

It was such a blast from the past to go through all my writing folders and old web files to find all these works for you. I know there are a lot of poems (like I said, main outlet of expression for most of my life), but I promise there is more here in this collection. There is something for everyone! This is, sadly, about half of my work! So, I decided to divide all my writing projects into two collections! I am not sure when the other one will be published, but rest assured, it will come to be. I also did not want to bore you with a 200+ collection with 77 poems (not including short ones and yes, I counted!)

The works in this collection are from my public school years, mostly high school. The earliest works I found were from age eight and they go until I graduated. Ah, puberty and hormones; the perfect crazy muses for writing! I also put them in time order and put the years I wrote them (if I could recall). Through these works, I hope you will learn more about my younger self that helped shape who I am today, what inspired/inspires me, how my writing evolved, and gives you a form of entertainment.

Thank you so much for being supportive of me and my work! All these little writings would be stuck in folders, but because of you, they are being allowed to shine like they should, since they are the stepping stones to the writing blessings I have now. As the title states, me becoming published all started out with these writings and a sweet, little dream . . .

Love,
Morgan Straughan Comnick

Poems

"Love is being willing to express every emotion all at once with no hint of fear or reason to why you do it. It is selfish. It is lonely. It is painful . . . It is the most beautiful thing one can experience."

—Morgan Straughan Comnick

This is the oldest work I could find. I was about eight years old when I wrote this! The spelling was *monstrous* and I'm still not sure if I was trying to write a poem or a short story! I made it a poem. I even had a drawing at the end of it! Gosh! Still, I am fond of this first work of mine. It makes me smile to remember being so innocent and believing in magic. Lucky for me, this never left me.

My Little Box (1997)

I went to the Attic
And then, I saw a box
For me, one and all

Inside was all mine
Dresses and other things
Most of all, something neat happened
My book collection happened to be complete

I read a book in that minute
It was red, old, and dusty.
Then, I fell into a Dreamland.
I dreamed I was a little princess
Walking along a rusty, old castle in France.
I left the castle at half past nine.
Then, I saw a man by a ship in baggy underpants.
He sailed me to New York and it happened.
I saw my papa, waiting for me.
I gave him a hug and kiss
We sailed to the castle in the mist.
Then I got out of Dreamland in time for dinner.

It's been 20 years since I saw that old box
It's in my attic now
My daughter cleaned it
She said she was Heidi
And later, she woke up by that big, old box
Book in hand.

This was in an old diary I had. I wrote this as a song after reading a poem and listening to my, at the time, favorite band, 3LW, a lot. I wrote this sometime in middle school for I recall having *Yu-Gi-Oh!* posters all around me when I was writing it. I'm sure it was inspired by a boy, but I can't remember now! HA! I was really proud of this and used to sing it like a song.

Your Eyes (2002)

Oh, boy, you stare at me
And I only watch you shyly.
Distance: that's all it is
But, I feel something for you.

I'm always in your embrace.
I know your warmth, that comfort.
We need to become one,
Yet you were my friend first

Until, you made my knees weak with those . . .

Those things that shine,
Those things that mesmerize.
Those things that sparkle,
Those things that seem to hypnotize.

Oh, I'm trapped in the spell, the spell of . . . your eyes.

Sweetie, what'd you do to me?
You've always been fine,
Yet now I get butterflies.
I'd fight any girl to make you mine.

Oh help, tell me why!

You're always wandering my dreams.

Give me our special smile (secret).
Now, I always blush.
You make me think my life's worth living.

This wouldn't have happened if I didn't look into your
crystal pools,
the color of those . . .

Those things that shine,
Those things that mesmerize.
Those things that sparkle,
Those things that seem to hypnotize.

Oh, I'm trapped in the spell, the spell of . . . your eyes.

I want our lips to melt together.
I imagine holding hands, flying away.
Then, you tell me the words
And I respond to you. It's our day!

Oh, I need you, want you, love you!

Those things that shine,
Those things that mesmerize.
Those things that sparkle,
Those things that seem to hypnotize.

Oh, I'm trapped in the spell, the spell of . . . your eyes.

I see you and me in perfect harmony.

Our hearts are one, our souls having fun.
A past, future, so lovely and true,
in those, baby your . . .

Those things that shine,
Those things that mesmerize.
Those things that sparkle,
Those things that seem to hypnotize.

Oh, I'm trapped in the spell, the spell of . . . your eyes.

Oh thanks to . . . your eyes!

I was assigned in my freshman language class to look at an object and write a poem about it. I looked at this green froggie blanket my brother had forever (it was made for him when he was super small) and this all came to me. My grandmother who made it passed away a few years earlier. I am dedicating this to you, Grandma Aggie.

The Warmth of Colors (2004)

Alone in the darkness,
Listening to the rain pour,
Shivering to the thunder,
Needing your hug more.

Cuddling my knees,
My heart in despair.
Why did you leave me?
I thought you cared!

Then, I see you,
Hanging out of clutter.
The colors, so lovely,
With a note: "To me love grandmother"

I stare at your work.
The frogs: so smiley and bright.
I actually smile,
The first time tonight.

You're wrapped around me,
Your embrace so warm.
We sit on our bed
Watching the rain still pour.

Light is in my heart now.
I do have a friend, no fear.
You may have died,
But you're still here.

I wrote this the summer after my freshman year in summer school, the summer I discovered *Sailor Moon* . . . Boy! How my life has changed! I initially wrote it for the couples of *Sailor Moon*, but I had a small crush on a boy then too and claimed it was for him. Although now, I will admit, it was for the best couples of *Sailor Moon*, one of the shows that changed my life! ☺

My Love (2004)

Rose petals fall from the skies
When you first arrive.
You're never late to save me,
you're always on time
Every one wants you
Cause, baby, you're *so* fine!
But, why can't I ask you:
Will you be mine?

You're always in my mind, my thoughts.
You're with me when I'm in bed.
And every time I see you,
My face turns bright red!
Your eyes always spark,
Your face always shine.
Your heart is so pure,
And you're just too kind!

When you hug me,
My heart is about to bust
When you grab my hand,
I wish it could last forever; it must!
My dream is to have
a magical first kiss.
Would you do it?
Or would you diss

I know we're different.
I know I'm not special, but let my heart dance.
I know you could do better,
But please, babe, I'd love a chance.

I know we're close friends,
But notice my feelings, with all your might.
You are my shooting star;
I'll wish on your light.

I bet you think I'm crazy
Writing, thinking, all this stuff,
But when I see you, the words . . .
Write themselves; I know it's not much.
We're from two different worlds
And I haven't known you for long,
But I must get this feeling out
Before you may be gone

It's true!
I'll say it: I'm deeply in love with you!
And maybe, Oh if only maybe . . .
You love me too!

Another creative writing assignment, but I was thinking of hauntings and spirits a lot at the time due to *Spirit Vision* being born in my mind. I dedicate this to every spirit, known and unknown, I have encountered, and to all the angels who watch over me. I love you all.

Dearest Angel (2004)

A sender of God.
A holder of peace.
A wish come true,
yet, you seem out of reach.
A smile of pure love,
A face of true happiness.
I wish for your hand of healing ways
And a simple butterfly kiss.

You play with me.
You make me feel like magic is real.
Yet, you run away from me.
How does that make me feel?
Don't be scared;
I want to be your friend.
We're not so different at all.
I want to be with you until my end.

I know people say bad things about you.
I know that people scream at you.
It's just that people don't understand you.
They don't try to know you,
But . . . Not me
I know you have no body of your own.
I'll accept you for who you are.
You were human once.
Why do people treat you so hard?

Your heart deserves a crown of stars
And winds of gold.
Your hair is so lovely,

More than they told.
Take my hand, trust me!
I care for you dearly.
I'll always believe in you and spirits no matter what
Your heart is still here; it's inside me!

"You block my sun, outshine my moon, and shatter my beautiful stars." - Morgan

Ah ... Summer drama camp! One of the best parts of my summers! Our director is an idol of mine to this day! He wrote an amazing musical for us and we learned it all in four days! We had such fun! I wrote this during it and I dedicate it to my theater camp pals and my director! You guys rock! BTW: My character's name was Anita Mann ... See if you get the joke! ☺

Mystery (2004)

A mystery comes for tonight,
A killer roams around.
They've given us quite a fright,
No clues are found.

Death is looking for us.
Chills going down our spines.
Will we last until dusk?
All we can do is wait for our time.

We have a mystery
Who could it be?
Yes, the tension is building, you see?
It's all for one; that's the key!

I wanna scream like crazy.
I gotta get out of here!
It's really easy to see
That I'm in total fear!

We'll search for this faker.
I have so much; I gotta live!
I won't meet my maker yet;
You won't take me!

Hold on for your life!
We have to solve the mystery.
Try with all your might,
Or we'll be history!

Solve it . . .
Solve it . . .
Solve it . . .
Live it . . .

Another poem I wrote in theater camp and also to thank my director, Rick, for allowing me to be in my first play that summer as well (*The Beetles': Yellow Submarine*. I was Penny Lane. Rick wrote the whole musical). I love acting and I hope this shows it.

Time to Shine! (2004)

Flashing lights,
sight of the stage.
The eagerness of the crowd,
My nervous daze.

The director's voice,
The final call.
The rising bows,
The curtains withdraw.

Ready, set, go!
It's my time to shine!
I'll show no fear!
This moment will be mine!

I wrote this to one of my loving *Cardcaptor Sakura* site sisters for her birthday, but I want to dedicate it to all my sisters and close friends in my Sakura and Li's Dream Cloud days. All the fun and work we did together still makes me smile! You guys are gems!

Sister (2005)

Name as sweet as cinnamon,
Arms delicate like a dove.
Spirit that soars like a butterfly,
A heart flying on the wings of love.

Beauty indescribable,
Your name replaces it.
Talents shining above the rest;
Yourself a world-wide gift.

Kiss as precious as a cloud,
Scent blowing like lilacs.
Ivory hair more fair than the night sky,
So loveable, you want her back.

The moon reflects off your gorgeous smile,
Eyes sparkling like a crystal cave.
An elegant figure swims in life's pool,
She is the sun of the day.

Walk along fair maiden.
Grace the Earth and you will be missed.
My support, my friend, my love,
You are my sis.

Time for my nerd to show! I had just discovered *InuYasha* and what I tend to do with shows I love is my mind makes characters for them! I made a character named Aino and this poem/song is supposed to reflect her and be her imagery theme song. A little embarrassing to admit, but I really liked how it turned out. The reason it does not rhyme is because I figured it would be sung mostly in Japanese if it was real, so why spend the time making English rhymes?

Prove My Heart Can Shine (2005)

I dream my life will soon be understood
My pressure will lure my heart
Let my soul fly free
And untangle my destiny
Allow the warmth to fill my veins
Allow the skies to hear my cry
Break the glass, loosen the chains
Let the sand lead me to my hour

Someday . . . It'll be time
My time to shine above the rest
My time to show my light
Let my feelings glow in the night
and prove my heart can shine

Cherry blossoms guide the path
to reveal my spirits lifting
the silver moon changes the wind
that blows my hair with gentle gold
I can almost see the girl I want to see
Crystal pools splash my clouded eyes
Clearing the dragon's fire
Allowing me to sing the praise

Someday . . . It'll be time
My time to shine above the rest
My time to show my light
Let my feelings glow in the night
and prove my heart can shine

My past circles my mind
Unknown memories knot me to despair
Thoughts and power feed off my courage
Shine, twinkle, glitter my little hopes
My guardian butterfly flaps her wings
to whisper my heart's longing answers
My friends love me; please find me
I'll always smile, be cheery; I now know
I'm the star that kisses my darling and heals my heart

It's now my time to shine
Like a star shining in the dark sky called life
It's time to shine, prove my heart can shine

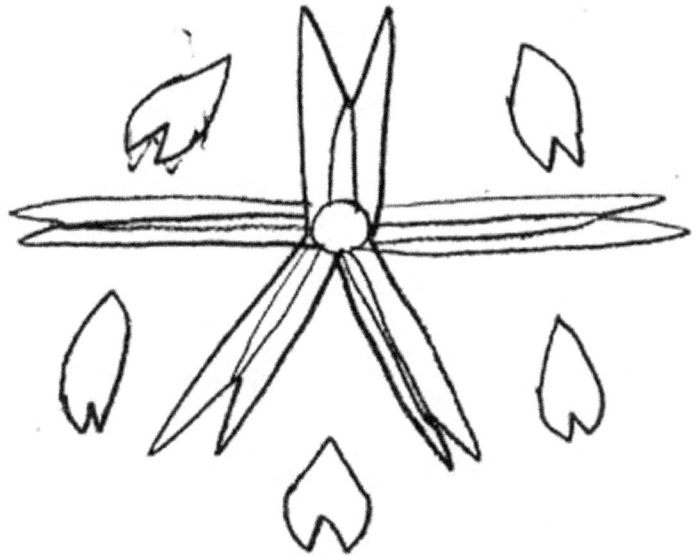

I needed a confidence boost since everyone thinks (even to this day) that I am so helpless and innocent. I wrote this song for this reason. I still catch myself singing this song randomly. This is one of my poems I would record as a song and love doing it if I ever got a record deal (ha!). I want everyone to know they are strong and can do amazing things, no matter what others tell them!

Watch and See (2005)

I may not be a super girl
I just live in the normal world
Living to the beat of life
Not following my heart's advice
The wind that hits me in the face
Is the breath of my words' disgrace
This tasteless breeze is so cold
Not as sweet as my mind had told
I'm a shadow trapped in the night
I want to get out with all my might

Gotta Jump
Gotta Fly
Gotta reach up for the sky
I'm so high, you'll never, ever catch me
Gotta feel
Gotta dance
Gotta give my dreams a chance
Don't believe me? Then watch and see

The path I took made me such a fool
My mind tricked me; how cruel!
Now I know my heart was right
And I'm willing to take the fight
Fantasy felt like a kiss
But reality was hard to miss
What exactly should I do?
Whatever it is, I'll prove it to you

Gotta Jump
Gotta Fly

Gotta reach up for the sky
I'm so high, you'll never, ever catch me
Gotta feel
Gotta dance
Gotta give my dreams a chance
Don't believe me? Then watch and see

The truth seems so far
Even with the help of a star
It feels like I'm going to fall
But, that's not the story at all
I know I'm not strong, as you can see
But, I'm driven by the taste of victory
I've put this fear off for too long
I'll destroy it & prove you wrong!

Gotta Jump
Gotta Fly
Gotta reach up for the sky
I'm so high, you'll never, ever catch me
Gotta feel
Gotta dance
Gotta give my dreams a chance
Don't believe me? Then watch and see

I wrote this to my neighbor, dear friend, and inspiration, Josh. We have the same birthday, so we call each other twin. He got me a *Spongebob* notebook to write my poems in along with a song he wrote for me. I have filled many pages of this gift with my work. Thanks twin!

Who is a Hero? (2006)

A hero is someone you look up to.
Some have fancy capes, catchy names,
Super special powers too,
And like to play "hero vs. villain games."

But, that's not the true meaning . . .

A hero is bold, brave, pure,
Kind, helpful, always there,
Has many wonderful gifts,
And is any and everywhere.

By this meaning, it's easy to see,
You are a hero . . . and mine.
Thank you, for always helping me,
From now until the end of time.

I was bored working at my mom's shop one day and my mind drifted to my brother and I sitting by the bay window when it would rain so hard, we would lose power for our Sega and we would sing until the power came back. This is to that memory, a memory of rainy days every child, I am sure, can relate to.

A Child's Rainy Day (2005)

Little one of my eye
Sits by the window
Watching his tears hit the glass
Feeling life on the go

Lightning strikes your face
Scaring your gentle hopes
Thunder shakes your heart
Making you hate love most

Water rushing over the grass
Clouds as gray and sad as you
You want to go out and laugh
Yet you can't stop what you do

Smile, my darling
The sun will rise
The rain will leave, for you
And you can play, jump high, in the sky!

It was snowing the last day before Christmas break and this all came to me. I love Christmas so much and I hope this poem explains why and how much.

My Favorite Signs (A Christmas Poem) (2005)

Santa Claus wrapping gifts,
Gentle snowflakes falling from the sky,
Puppies snuggled in warm blankets . . .
It must be Christmas time!

Holly, wreaths, candles a glow,
Grandma baking yummy cookies with chips.
Shopping for our loved ones,
And mistletoe making us kiss on the lips.

Getting to wear my fur coat,
Making lots of popcorn and hot cocoa.
Decorating the beautiful, shining tree,
And all the parties . . . Let's Go!

Telling enchanted tales to my cousins,
Singing and dancing to Christmas songs.
Watching a snowman and red-nosed reindeer,
And getting out of school for so long.

Yet, the best thing about the holidays
is celebrating it with my loved ones and all who come.
Blessing Lord Jesus on his holy star
And my dear memories of Christmas fun.

Ah! Now comes the *Love Era of Morgan's poems*! I met Derrick through a mutual friend at the end of 2004 and we began dating on December 3rd, 2004. Well, since Derrick's last name is Comnick, like my married name, you can assume we got married! ☺ Yep! I'm a lucky lady who found her true love in high school. So, I was love struck with puppy-eyed thoughts of this boy all the time. So, I went through an era of only writing love poems! Here is poem #1.

I See Now (2005)

I never knew why you loved me
I never understood why I fell for a stranger
I never remember happiness without you
I never was so willing to risk hurt and danger

You give me motivation to try my best
You love me unconditionally
You gave my life color, made it amazing
You fully understand me

If I lost you, my cheerfulness would die
My world would be only gray
Life would stop breathing or moving
There would be no special days

My love, I have nothing to hide from you
My dear, I have more confidence
My babe, you make me feel like the only one
My life, you allow me to open the fence

You are my shining star, my drug, my craving
When we are gone, our bodies will die
Our spirits soar to heaven and then,
Our souls, shining stars, ready to fly

You caught my heart and soul; hook, line, and sinker
My heart will always be inside our hugs
Don't cry, destroy the pain of separation
I see now, I know now . . . you are my true love

Love poem #2. Derrick got me a promise ring for our first anniversary and it was such a huge deal. EVERYONE knew before I did (even my mom)! It was a little silver band with a pearl in the middle and two almost impossible to see diamonds on the side. I loved this ring, but soon after, the pearl fell off and I was crushed. I was so scared to tell him but when I finally did, he was so kind and understanding. That's when I knew what love was. That is when I wrote this.

Symbol of our Love (early 2006)

On a cold day in early December
One of the greatest days of my life
God's purest angel gave me a gift, a ring
That made my heart fill with delight

It was the color of perfection
With diamonds shining like the moon
And a pearl, white and angelic as the sea
It was a sign that you loved me through and through

I treasure this ring as I do you
It shows our hearts are now one
Yet, nature was cruel and I was foolish
The pearl was gone, what have I done?!

Yet, you smiled at me with sparkling eyes
And used a gentle touch, which was the best
You told me something that stopped my tears:
"I love you too much to love you less."

Yet, my heart craves to make it up to you
You are my angel from above
Oh sweetheart, I love you so much
And this ring, I know, is a symbol of our love

Love poem #3. I was looking at a key in my mom's shop and it reminded me of Derrick! How sad?! It also reminded me of all the amazing things that can be unlocked if you have the right key.

Frozen Still (2006)

There's a place,
Holding a golden key.
It opens a silver lock,
With amazing things to see.

Desires, pleasures, fun . . .
Passions, dreams, hopes . . .
Memories, goals, stories . . .
All the things we love most

Lifeless it all is, illusions.
yet you have to stare.
It makes you glow,
Reliving these cares.

This elegant place is tainted.
It's too perfect; it has proof,
For if you savor happiness . . .
you don't wanna go back to truth.

Yet, I want to take you there,
My love who is mine . . .
I only want to be embraced in your arms,
Frozen still, frozen in time.

Love poem #4. It's amazing how grossly in love I was, huh?

Love is not the Word (2006)

Object of my heart's desire
Key to my happiness
My life, my glory
My shining star, my love

When your heart aches, I cry
If you are hurt, I feel the pain
When you smile, I glow inside
When you love, I love back

Sparkling eyes that reflect forest beauty
Hands as sweet and gentle as a cloud
A smile worth more than any priceless gem
And a heart that is greater than gold

Darling, I love you more than you'll know
You are my better half
You have stolen my heart
And become my soul

Love is not the word I use anymore
To describe these beautiful emotions
When I am asked "What is love?"
I say your name.

I was having a really bad day in math and my teacher, who sadly showed favoritism to the max, refused to help me and refused to let my friends near me help either. I have never been good at math and this really stung because I tried my hardest at everything. I wrote this instead and it helped all the feelings of failure and worthlessness flow out.

Girls Know Nothing (spring 2006)

In the playground of my youth
Children are yelling about a pointless thing
The girls run and scream in fear
As the boys chase and say, "girls know nothing"

I smile to myself, listening
Hearing those three words again
But, I know more than people credit
Where to possibly begin . . .

I know how to tie my shoes, button a coat
I know what hobbies I love most
I can clean my room, cook, and babysit
and say "thank you" and "please" to my host

I can write and read
I am blessed with the power to see
They taught me how to show respect
I can say my abc's and sing my do, re, mi's

I know to tell when the weather is bad or fair
I can keep a hot dog in its bun
I can beat any boy at a video game
And hey, girls just want to have fun!

I understand more than people think
I have and know how to cherish myself
I am a person who feels emotions
And know that I have true love with no help

I wrote this for Derrick to congratulate him on graduating (he barely did since he disliked school work so much). I was so proud of him. I made a fancy, framed copy for him and he has it hanging up by our bed now still. I dedicate this to Derrick, Evan, Nathan, and all the other Farmington High school graduates of 2006! Thanks for leading the way for us!

The Graduate I'm Proud Of (May 2006)

The band plays your march
The crowd is in an excited daze
You and your friends walk in proudly
Showing an uncertain gaze

You're dressed in your gown
It's your night to shine
Sitting, playing with your tassel
Thinking that it's almost time

The school song is sung
While candles are aglow
I am filled with happiness for you
Yet also a little woe

The usher motions you to rise
You walk up to the stand
You finally got your diploma
You did it my darling man!

I see your mom happily crying,
Your dad has a sweet smile.
And even your brother
is watching for a while.

Confetti fills the air
Silly string is sprayed
Graduation caps are thrown
Today is your day!

I'm shaking and holding back tears
The future is yours and goes to above
I have grown honored for you:
The graduate I'm proud of.

"Tick, tock, I rule the Clock!"
Morgan

Now we get out of the love poems and more into the transition poems. Derrick is now graduated and I am a senior in high school. Although I had tons of fun, but sometimes, loneliness, frustration, and stress kicked in, causing some interesting poems. Thank gosh I had my writing to vent so I could enjoy my year! ☺ This poem really boosted my confidence in writing. It won second place in our school's annual poetry café out of 54 entries! I got a free t-shirt and it was displayed in a trophy case for a while. My best friend made me read it and I was so nervous! Still, this is an honor to me.

Even I Can . . . (2006)

Even a sun can shed tears
Even a melody can rip you in two
Even a raindrop can burn your spirits
Even time can lock you within fear

Even I can frown
I can lose my shine
Lose it to the shadow of hate
Not even a sparkle to show

Even I can bleed
When no cut is found
It hurts, blackens poison
Stabs my heart still

Even I can cry
The dragon of mist around me
Burning my pride
Melting my soul alive

Why stare?
Lies are my only memories
You'll never understand
What you stole from me

I was, am happy
But, now, there's no reason to try
I'll smile again soon
but, I wanna let you know . . .

Even I can feel pain.

This is a poem I wrote for a local band, The Dead Pawns. They changed it a little to make the lyrics flow better, but here is the original. I have not chatted with them since when MySpace was popular (I wonder if anyone knows what I'm talking about), but I want to give them and every band who never gives up their dream a shout out!

Willing to Try (2006)

I see the clearing
With the help of the haze
My mind ever rocking
In an unsteady daze

The wheels are turning
Creating a motion
Sealed inside my soul
With my ever devotion

Spinning, reeling, I feel the vibe
Tossing, turning, in the dead of night
Watching, waiting, for my chance
Struggling, fighting, with all my might

My words may die
I will lock up my cries
I'm making a change this time...
Let's get willing to try.

Some call me evil
But, they're all insane
Beating themselves up,
Scared of life's little game

The pit of downfall
Swells up inside
But, my hope is sparkling
And I'm ready to fly

Spinning, reeling I feel the vibe
Tossing, turning, in the dead of night
Watching, waiting for my chance
Struggling, fighting, with all my might

Oh, the battle may be bloody
Hey, but we must get burned by the fire
To truly make a stand, oh yeah
We feel the victory of pain and desire

My words may die
I will lock up my cries
I'm making a change this time . . .
Let's get willing to try.

Oh yeah . . . let's all try . . . woo!

on the wings of fun!

Also in my fun and stressful senior year, I had a lot of down time (three study halls, although I did take several college classes). So, I wrote a lot from boredom. These poems would come to me at once and my pencil would flow on its own. I am sure that deep down inside, I needed to write these, but most of the time, I couldn't tell you why. This one I know I wasn't feeling pretty so this came out of my pencil. Enjoy the first Boredom poem.

I Want to be Beautiful (2006)

Sitting here, thinking in the still silence
Deciding to write my dreams
I want to list all things beautiful
For I can never be one it seems

A tiger lily flower in bloom
A couple snuggling in the snow
A kiss or hug from a loved one
Christmas candles and lights aglow

The cute person sitting next to me
A sweet, innocent babe
The moon shining in the night
A puppy wanting to play

The sunset, the sunrise
The sweater my grandma made
The value of friendship
And waking up to a nice day

To me, many things, people, and things are lovely
Though I think I am not
My loved ones give life a reason to be beautiful
Saying I am too, their final thought

Boredom poem #2. I must have been watching someone . . .

All I can do is Observe You (2006)

Why do I get nervous when he walks into my life?
Why do I pray he repays my simple, loving favors?
Why do I get worried I'll be caught if I only think about
him?
Why does only his smile stick out in my mind?
And his eyes twinkle with the stars at night?
You are my guide.
All I can do is observe you.

I was thinking about *Spirit Vision* again and this is what happened in study hall!

Blinded

A year apart, but it's not easy to tell
The biggest smile I've ever viewed
And a gentle nature to match
Yet, I can't get the clue

Sparkling large eyes showing your kindness
Raven hair that reflects the noon sun
A clumsy, fun-loving creature
Yet, why did this feeling have to come?

My protector when I am weak
My friend when I am invisible
An innocent one who enjoys life
Whose hug creates a fire to warm my soul

I know this feeling called love
For I feel it for another
But, I am clouded by a similar emotion
You feel more important than a brother

To me, a boy I hardly know
Make my dreams sweeter while lying in bed
Is it possible to be good and love two
I'm not sure for my heart has made me blinded

Another *Spirit Vision* based poem I wrote in language class, although this is one for events that has not happened yet in the series . . . Hmmm . . .

Now That You're Gone (2006)

Oh, I remember when fate smiled down
Having only us in mind
After all the hardships we have suffered
Are now blocked by sacred time

I don't understand
How can this be?
It was written in the stars
That you're my destiny

Now that you're gone
I only cry
Now that you're gone
My words all die
Now that you're gone
I became shy
and lost all my pride
I wanted to be your tomorrow, not yesterday
But now you're gone

Although you're right next to me
Our minds are worlds away
Your heart is lost and can't recall
Our happy loving days
Why did evil make this come?
It's impossible to be true.
Even though you may be made of darkness
You always told me "I love you"

Our past circles cruelly

Making the future unclear
I fall with my love
Being destroyed by fear

My will strongly fights
To gain your memory of us again
Please try for me
Because deep down, we know love will win

Now that you're gone
I only cry
Now that you're gone
My words all die
Now that you're gone
I became shy
and lost all my pride
I wanted to be your tomorrow, not yesterday
But now you're gone

Come back to me, someday soon . . .
Don't be gone

"Awesome Sauce home skillet biscuit!"

This poem represents two events: a close guy friend of me and Marissa's moved out of nowhere and they had a spat right before this. I was originally trying to prove how valuable our time with someone is. Then, soon after this, a classmate of ours passed away in a car accident. This boy was one of the first ones who gave me the confidence to talk to boys by poking innocent fun at me. So, I changed the poem to honor him as well. I still recall how his mother hugged me at his visitation when I thanked her son for giving me confidence, although I had never met her before then. Sometimes, when someone slips away, you need an anchor who understands the storm you are in the middle of.

He Slipped Away (2006)

Who says friends do not fight?
It is an unpleasant part of life.
It may be the only way to see
How valuable friendship takes flight

All I want is to see your face once more:
Twinkling eyes, a unique voice, and clever taste
Giving, fun, caring, brave, passionate, a protector
Who always loved and smiled; that was your choice.

Yet, a lightning bolt shocked my soul
when I heard you were gone.
How could you leave so suddenly?
I felt I did the most evil of wrongs.

When I felt your final embrace
I did not want to let go of you, part of my world
Bathed in shining light, you faded like an angel
I held in my tears to prove I am your strong girl

We were so close to victory
Before unforeseen fate took you away.
Yet, my guardian, destiny will guide us . . .
So we can see you again, someday . . .

I wrote this a few years earlier during my freshman year. We lost a classmate to suicide. She was fourteen. It is hard to stomach, being that young, but it was not my first brush with young death. When I was ten, we lost a classmate who got a rope swing accidently wrapped around his neck and he suffocated to death right before the helicopter came. This one hit me hard because I saw him the day before. He smiled and asked me to play with him; I didn't and it still haunts me. I think this event, this guilt, led me to my fascination with spirits. Secretly, I was looking for him to tell him I was sorry every recess I ever had, every time I walked down an empty hall.

My freshman year, after the suicide, I began to think about how these two young people will never have a family, never get married, never even graduate . . . That is when I wrote this, back in November 2003.

After my friend died in a car crash my senior year (he is the one I wrote "He Slipped Away" for), I dug this poem out, painful as it was, and made two copies of it. We had baskets on two empty chairs at the back of our graduation ceremony for them. I placed a flower and a copy of the poem with a personal note from me on each chair for their families. I have no idea if they got it, but if so, I hoped it made the day a pinch easier.

This poem is special and difficult for me, so I dedicate this poem to the following people, along with every other person who did not see their high school graduation due to a tragic, young death: Ray House, Lindsey Dann, Cole Dillon, Drew Killon, Clint Lee, and Brad Lewis. FHS loves you all.

Invisible Graduate (2007)

The first step into the world,
A night we'll always remember.
Yet, something is missing
and it's been gone forever since November.

The day fate stabbed you
and took you up away.
The shock when I heard the news
that eventful November day.

Everyone is excited in their seats
waiting to hear my speech.
Yet, I wish you were here to listen:
Why are you so far out of my reach?

I walk up to the platform,
Shaking to see all the people in the crowd.
A final deep breath and smile
before I tell about the person I know now.

I remember your humor, your smile,
Your loving kindness and gentle grace.
You would never let anyone be alone.
To you, "everyone had a place."

I know you would not want us to be sad
Yet, we all wish you were here.
I can almost feel your presence
Being extremely near

Flowers are in your chair
In honor of your memory.
Suddenly, a wind blows them off,
Setting your spirit free.

The principal states we're graduated
Cheers are let out by every young woman and man
And you are here celebrating with us:
My friend and ours . . .

Another boredom and stress poem. It has sort of a yin-yang message.

I Will Never go any Further (2007)

Someday when you are gone
I will long for you, very long
Staring at the empty sky; hollow and bare
Allowing my mind to wander and care

The world was green, but not special; a fear
The sky is blue, but will never be clear
Beauty will exist, but is merely a reflection in a mirror
The earth was only truly beautiful with you here

I can see through the thickest fog, known as tall
Walk into the darkness like it's nothing at all
I am not scared anymore of death's call
And I am willing to take the final fall

You, who is my gentle touch, come again
For someday, you'll become my guiding wind
I cry at the thought on the inside
As an angel, you will fade away to fly

I will continue to walk as a body not filled
But, my spirit will vanish as you willed
When this happens, I'll be lost, but stronger
Yet, since you are gone, I will never go any further

This is my: I FINALLY SNAPPED poem, so anyone mentioned here, I apologize! I recall this day. It was one of the roughest of my public school life and it seemed every boy hated me or was making my life worse. Some freshmen boys were being overly stupid and immature when I was waiting for my dad to pick me up (I know . . . a senior without a license . . . blasphemy!). I had enough and as I glared at them, I wrote this in my head and wrote it down once I got home. Not sure how I feel about this poem, but hey! Everyone has bad days, right?

P.S. Derrick and I were on a short month break at the time, so he is sadly the ex I am referring to, but it did not last long and everything was smooth sailing after that.

Boys are Idiots (2007)

As I sit here silently,
bent over in pain from my "girl time"
I notice a group of freshmen
boys, being stupid.
One is spitting on the floor,
another talks like a rapper,
a skateboarder has his underwear fully shown.
I blink at their actions.
The flirts, the gross, the annoying
I am NOT in the mood
To look at this opposite gender!
My best friend was right: boys are idiots . . .
My guy friends are idiots for not comforting me.
My ex-boyfriend is an idiot for being so irresponsible.
My new crush is an idiot for being so dense.
My big brother is an idiot for forgetting my birthday.
My little brother is an idiot for siding with my ex over
me
and getting two dates to Sweetheart when I can get
none.
My cousin is an idiot for smoking in front of me at
Christmas.
Freshmen boys are stupid because . . . well, they just
are!
Oh look. One got in trouble
for punching his friends in the nuts.
I wish my dad would hurry . . .
He told me a girl can only trust her daddy and her dog.
I love my dog Lancey.
He's cuter and sweeter than any boy.
But, who will love me when he dies?
No boy will, even if there is a 'not idiot' one.
I always have my daddy . . .

80

but, he can't love me LIKE THAT.
We don't live in ancient times now!
Now they're giving each other piggy back rides.
Marissa was right.
Maybe being single is okay . . .
I don't need a guy!
I have a plan for my future
Yet, I feel numb, hollow, teary, empty.
But, I used up a year's worth of tears in one night.
God, what did I do to deserve this?
I go to church, I'm nice and forgiving.
I can change. Oh Gabriel!
Give me a sign!
Get me away from these howling monkeys.
Oh thank you! My dad's here.
Stupid boys, whistling at me when I pass.
Dumb law of nature, making guys cute.
But, I'm cheery. Who would like ugly me?
Stop being stupid, freshmen!
I wish I noticed sooner
that boys are idiots!

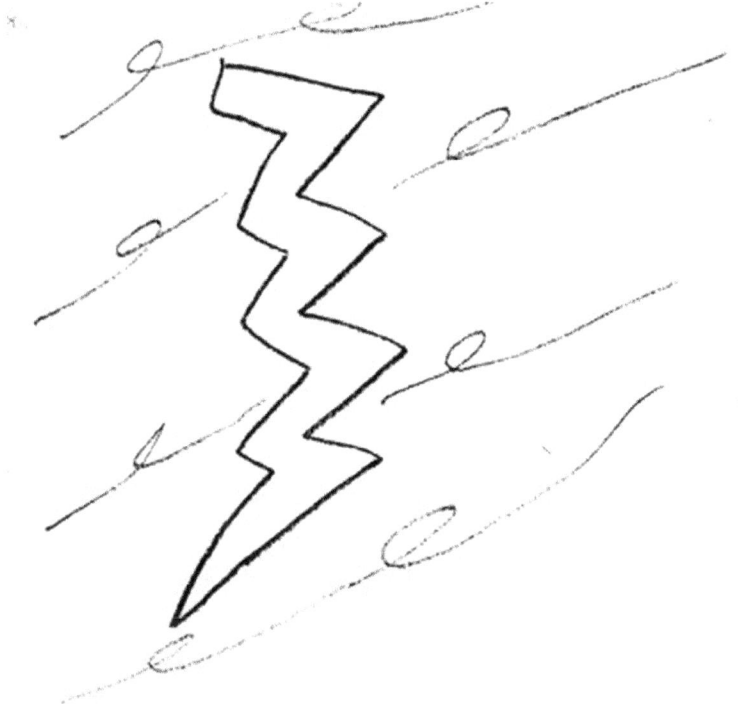

AH! The pain of waiting! This poem's for you!

Painful Game (2007)

How much will I suffer?
When will it end?
When will my answer come?
I want to be born again.

The wind hits my body forcefully,
Laughing in my tired face.
Making my heart pound crazily
and emotions hurt my case.

I cry at the sound of your name.
I feel sad when a girl is near.
I shake thinking of what you'll say.
Losing your friendship is my worst fear.

Please, give me a smile or a chance.
Babe, don't treat me the same.
Let me look at you once more
before we stop this painful game.

Boredom in study hall and loneliness in this one. Derrick was gone on a super long camping trip when I wrote this one and I was miserable.

Lonely Heart (2007)

Stuck in a frozen stand still
Shadows shield my eyes
Ashamed of my unknown sorrow
I wonder why I cry

Goose bumps control my body
Shivers crawl up my spine
My soul trapped in a whirlpool of despair
Let the pain stop in due time

I miss you, my beloved
The darling I need to hold
I wish you haven't left me
You were gone longer than told

Distance is between us
Space is making us be apart
Return soon, my love
I don't want to live with a lonely heart

I was a helper to a wonderful man and new language arts teacher. We had great conversations about Shakespeare, poetry, and book recommendations. He mostly worked with kids who failed language the previous year; it was sad how tickled pink he was that first day when he asked me if I knew who Robert Frost was . . . When he was lecturing, I wrote several poems that year. This one I based off a book of dreams I have and the nature and the beauty God has given us. I also did a different style with it. Can you see the pattern?

Nature's Lesson (2007)

Autumn fills the air with warm toned specks
Beauty foretells our happy union
Candles flicker in the night sky
Dancing to the news of each babe's birth
Embrace the coming of the day
Face it with caution and love
God has blessed you with this gem
Heaven then drops the gift from above
Ivy grows to protect the child
Justice will also stop the world's wrong
Kiss the compassion blowing in the wind
Light guides the path of life that's long
Magic enchants the forest green
Night shields evil's misdeeds
Open yourself to a revelation of the soul
Paint the everlasting desires you need
Quail not to the glorious Lord
Remember the power he shows
Sing the praise as a simple thanks
Take the road of life and get set to go
Undo the evils clouding your mind
Victory will rise then from the flames
Water cools your questioning spirit
X-ray your babe to win the game
Yet, understand the most important part
Zero is the loneliest number to the heart

Like the title suggests, I was stressed here and bored in art class. There you go.

Stress (2007)

Stress can make life unbearable
Emotions become misunderstood
Pure judgment vanishes
Simple things make the soul heavy and no good

School work piles, engrossing
Family's fight, making you feel small
Love controls your thoughts, burying one's being
Basic needs drive one up the wall

It's not selfish to worry about your needs
The world is not meant to crush
It's meant to comfort and help do what you do
So relax, enjoy yourself and life can't be rushed

Be an orphan, be single, be lazy
For a moment, only care about your happiness
Close your eyes and see
Then, believe and give freedom a kiss . . .

Another boredom poem. I even got my schedule out and wrote a line for each of my classes on it. This sums up what I have learned in high school.

A Reason (2007)

I study to challenge my fate
Sing to make life beautiful
Listen to music for the honor of others
I sit to help my friends
Cook to express my desire to live
Practice to learn my emotions
Watch to see how others view
I age to survive
Work to make someone smile
Embrace to better know myself
Laugh to see my true friends
Read to thank people for talent
Try to get to someday
Do art to appreciate splendor
Everything has a reason towards life
That is what school taught me

I had a big choice to make and this poem helped me with this. Also wrote it during down time in study hall.

Current Feelings (2007)

Tears in my eyes
Lump wedged in my throat
Body sickly pale
Voice locked fearing I'll choke

Swirling butterflies flutter inside
Heart beats in frozen time
Chaos of thoughts fly like shooting stars
Shaking into an unbreakable bind

Save me Lord, my beloved God
Lift my guilt on wings, away
Help me find peace and love
So I can see the light of day

We were outside, in my survivor advance college English composition class (we started out with thirteen and ended up with four by the end of the year), reading *King Lear* in the sunshine. It was a lovely day. I was listening to the sounds of the construction site (they were adding on to our building for the next year . . . of course we miss the good stuff) and this came to me. This made me think about how I got sick not long before this and the thought occurred to me: what if I didn't wake up? Not in a morbid way, but what would I want to tell my loved ones? With the sounds of the construction and the sky perfect as I kept gazing at it, this is what I wrote.

What is sad or ironic, my 'cuz' was in that class with me and he seemed too sincere looking at the sky and joyous when we discussed the play; his passion was acting. He loved those days. I could never see him not be happy. Four years later, we found out he killed himself. It rocked everyone to the core. I had forgotten about how peaceful he was that day and now, as I write this for you guys, that thought is comforting. Maybe I knew that one day, we would all need that image of him smiling in the sunshine.

Don't Cry When I am Gone

When I am gone
Promise not to cry
For it is wasteful
Since I am at your side

Tears are not needed
Since life is a gift
I still feel you
We'll never drift

I fly, you walk
I shine, you glow
We are not different
Beyond what is told

Words express our universal love
Dawning on a restless new time
I am here to guide your troubles
Pushing you up life's difficult climb

Never be sorry, never be scared
Use your life at its needed pace
You'll know I am always here
And someday . . . we'll again embrace

We'll be together again . . . with the right tears

Outside again for *King Lear* and Virginia Tech had happened. I wrote this trying to process all of the confusion and utter hurt I was feeling. I dedicate this to anyone in that terrible situation.

I wish I could end with a higher note for my last poem, but all my other works are from my college days and after. They will be included in the next collection!

Thanks for sticking with me for so long! ☺

I Don't Understand

I don't understand why hurting occurs.
I can't see what it gains.
Does it make you feel better to dishonor yourself?
Is being powerful that rewarding?
Does being feared fill the loss of love?
You draw attention to yourself
So people will care like you want.
Do you hate this life so much that you leave it before
it's your time?
To me, that seems wasteful.
Why take innocent people with you?
Are you too scared to go alone? Yeah, that's why.
It can't fill that void in your heart.
But, will you end up in the same place?
How can you want to see their loved ones cry?
You chose that awful path.
Whoever thought of hurting was blind.
Who created weapons must have been made of ice.
Please, don't be remembered like that.
This world may be lonely, but don't cross over.
Before you go insane, you have a friend.
Someone who will care . . . That can be me.
All people have good . . . Please understand.

Scripts

"I am child*like*, not child*ish*. Mature in mind and actions, young in interests and spirit. This allows me to be anything I want to be. Why would you mock a gift like that?"

—Morgan Straughan Comnick

This had me in a giggle fit! I wrote this when I was . . . ten, so it must be my first script. All the characters are based on my cousins and Miles is my brother. We used to play together a lot at Grandma's. Now, the youngest, who was just born when I wrote this script, is in eighth grade! My gosh! I miss those happy, pleasant times. We always had a blast together. I was the oldest, hence why I wrote it. We even acted this out. It had a mystery title below it, so I guess it was meant to be a mystery . . . I never did finish it! Still, I hope you enjoy or at least smile at what I have.

*NOTE: I KNOW I am using thy totally wrong! I twitched at this, but I was just into medieval stories then so I'm assuming that was the only word I knew. I edited all the major problems, but I just couldn't bring myself to get rid of my ten-year-old thys. Bear with them please and enjoy the imagination of ten-year-old Morgan.

Act I

Scene: Court yard, playing badminton. The princesses and princes are playing. The king is sitting on a bench.

Everyone laughing.

PRINCESS BRIANA: Jordon, don't go and become a wild beast!

PRINCESS MORGANA: (laughs) Briana, hush thy talk to the child!

PRINCE AUSTINEGO: (screaming and pointing upward) Look! Up!

A random bird noise sounds.

PRINCESS BRIANA: Thy bird of winter . . . It is best to go, right Jordon?

PRINCE JORDON: Yeah (laughs)

KING MILES: (Laughing madly on his throne on the side of the court) The bird of feat will be thy soon!

Everyone trots on their invisible horses to have their dinner in the dining hall stage.

KING MILES: (In a loud, excited voice) Cooked swan! Yum!

PRINCESS MORGANA: Father, why kill thy swan? It is luck to thy kingdom aren't it not?

KING MILES: Because thy bird is *so* good!

PRINCESS BRIANA: Oh father!

PRINCE AUSTINEGO: (Tugging on Morgana's sleeve) Sissy! Colton!

PRINCE JORDON: Ah! Hello Colton! (waves)

SIR COLTON: (bows to everyone) Good afternoon. My Lord, I have thy news.

KING MILES: What have you brought?

SIR COLTON: Well, my Lord, thy Bold home is gone and Queen Marie is coming to stay over in thy castle next month.

KING MILES: Ah, thy Marie. She is a bloom in thy garden . . .

PRINCESS BRIANA and MORGANA roll their eyes.

PRINCESS MORGANA: Why does father like Marie?

PRINCESS BRIANA: She makes me sick! (She sticks her tongue outward)

PRINCESS BRIANA and MORGANA giggle.

KING MILES: (stands) Girls, it is music lesson time. To thy parlor. Go on now.

The girls curtsy and leave.

KING MILES: (snaps fingers twice, looking annoyed) Sir Colton.

SIR COLTON: (bows) Yes, my Lord?

KING MILES: Send Prince Austinego and Prince Jordon to thy play room.

SIR COLTON: (bows) Of course my Lord!

Act II

Scene: Music Parlor, the girls playing their instruments.

PRINCESS BRIANA: (says this while playing her harp) Aren't this song thy good?

PRINCESS MORGANA: (says this while playing her guitar) Yes . . . and hard!

PRINCESS BRIANA: (stops playing to look at Morgana) I agree (giggles)

KING MILES and SIR COLTON enter.

KING MILES: (looks at girls) Play.

The girls play their song.

KING MILES: Ah. Good thy daughters.

SIR COLTON: Good, my ladies (bows)

NOBLEMAN JONATHON enters.

NOBLEMAN JONATHON: My Lord. We're in thy festival tomorrow.

KING MILES: Very well.

PRINCESS MORGANA: Oh! That's so wonderful!

PRINCESS BRIANA: It's very grand.

KING MILES: Oh, yes indeed. (laughs)

SIR COLTON: I'm going to my chamber my Lord. (bows)

KING MILES: All right. Pleasant night to thy.

COLTON leaves.

NOBLEMAN JONATHON: May I take Jordon home, my king?

KING MILES: Of course. See you in thy morning.

JONATHON bows then leaves.

KING MILES: (facing the girls) Off to bed, daughters.

Girls kiss him on the cheek then exit.

Act III

Scene: Royal Chamber. Princesses are staring at their vanity.

PRINCESS BRIANA: (looking in the mirror) I must look pretty for thy festival.

PRINCESS MORGANA: (brushing hair) Fear not. You're beautiful enough.

PRINCESS BRIANA: Thank you. You are too.

PRINCESS MORGANA: (smiles at her) I will write in thy diary now.

PRINCESS BRIANA: I thy well.

The girls write in their diaries.

PRINCE AUSTINEGO: Night! (blows the girls kisses)

PRINCESS MORGANA: I'll tuck thy in. (tucks him into the littlest bed and kisses his cheek) Good night, thy little prince.

KING MILES enters.

KING MILES: Good night thy children (he kisses all of them on the forehead and leaves)

PRINCESS BRIANA: (hugs Morgana) Sweet dreams, dear sister.

PRINCESS MORGANA: (kisses the top of Briana's head) Wish to thy stars, best friend.

Girls go to their beds and say their prayers.

PRINCESS MORGANA and PRINCESS BRIANA: Protect thy kingdom with thy God. Amen.

PRINCESS MORGANA: (looks out the window) Look! A star! Make a wish!

PRINCESS BRIANA: I hope it comes true.

PRINCESS MORGANA: It thy will. It thy will . . .

Act IV

Scene: Kingdom Streets. Festival Day. Whole cast on the street.

NOBLEMAN MATTHEW: (blowing trumpet) Come royal sire! It's time.

KING MILES: Very well. Begin

Trumpet blows and everyone begins to march.

The next two scripts are very factual and sort of boring, but we had to do persuasive skits in my freshman communication arts class (This is a Mr. Banger assignment). I did this with Marissa, my best friend. I am for dogs. Read it and see who you think should win!

Also, the weird "cats and dogs can kill you thing," I actually looked up at the time and found those two things out. Not sure if they are true now, but it freaked me out at 15!

Which are Better Pets? Cats or Dogs? (2004)

One day, Leslie and Lauren were working on their debate assignment for English class when they thought of a topic about animals that would be good. They were deciding which was perfect: a cat or a dog. Leslie said cats were the best and Lauren said dogs were. They both had persuasive information on both.

LESLIE: Hey Lauren. I saw these cats at the Humane Society and they were like *so* cute! They look like they'd be the perfect pet for somebody.

LAUREN: That's after they clawed their last owner to death . . . (rolls eyes)

LESLIE: Well . . . I bet you can't think of another animal that's cute, innocent, and the best.

LAUREN: One animal and it's called A DOG!

LESLIE: Right and I'm supposed to believe this how?

LAUREN: Well, I do have a dog and cat and when I call the dog to come here, it listens.

LESLIE: The thing is when you do call your dog, it might just sit there sometimes with his tongue hanging out. I'm not trying to be mean, but it's like his brain is gone or something.

LAUREN: At least dogs listen unlike cats, who don't care about anything but their food.

LESLIE: That's not true! They do care about their owner, but thing is for sure is that dogs smell bad.

LAUREN: So do cats! You have to give dogs a bath to make them smell better.

LESLIE: Cats don't smell as bad and you give cats less baths than dogs if they're house cats.

LAUREN: (blinks, confused) Okay. Whatever.

LESLIE: Does your dog bark at night?

LAUREN: Yeah.

LESLIE: I'm not saying to get rid of your dog, but when your dog barks in the morning like at three a.m. some people might want to get some sleep and will be cranky.

LAUREN: Well, has your cat or anyone else's you know gone up a tree and you had to call the fire department to come get them down?

LESLIE: One of my friend's cats has. Why?

LAUREN: Like you said, I'm not saying to get rid of your cat, but if your cat didn't climb that tree, you wouldn't have to call the fire department to come get that crazy cat out of the tree. Maybe they would have time to do something more important.

LESLIE: Don't be so mean! I was only asking!

LAUREN: Sorry!

LESLIE: (Looks away then whispers) At least no one has to have a sign on their fence that says "BEWARE OF CATS!"

LAUREN: Well, you don't see cats sniffing out bombs and people out of buildings, do you?

LESLIE: Actually, no, but cats can heal!

LAUREN: WHAT?! Okay! This has gone too far.

LESLIE: I'm being serious about this! I found this out on the Internet by mistake.

LAUREN: How? I've never heard that before.

LESLIE: It's called cat purring! It heals injuries or at least helps them. I think that's what it said . . .

LAUREN: (rolls eyes) Right. Okay, I'll check that out later.

LESLIE: Okay, I'll give you the website later.

LAUREN: Okay! Now, dogs can sound the alarm for you when a burglary or an attacker comes at you before anyone gets injured, but cats are just quiet and won't warn you.

LESLIE: That's good sometimes though that a cat is quiet because what if you're working on something super important and you need concentration to work? A dog probably won't even be quiet for you.

LAUREN: That's true. Did you know cats can steal the oxygen while you're sleeping? They can jump on your bed and then on your chest right in front of your airway. Oxygen can't get through and you could die.

LESLIE: (looks up, thinking) That's sad, but you know dogs can cause death too. A dog owner could choke on the dog's salvia when it's giving you or their owner a wake-up lick or they lick their owner's face.

LAUREN: That's freaky. I guess both cats and dogs can cause death.

LESLIE: (nods) Yeah. At least a cat uses the litter box so you don't have to step in their crap, like dogs.

LAUREN: A litter box costs more than a newspaper and you can send the dog outside.

LESLIE: If you send a dog outside, it might dig up other dogs crap and that's just gross.

LAUREN: That would be gross, but not as gross as when a cat has a hairball.

LESLIE: That's gross too, but they're about the same in grossness. I'm not for sure because I haven't seen a dog dig up others' crap; I just heard my friend's dog does that sometimes. Let's get off that subject, that's just gross. Cats are more fun to play with.

LAUREN: (fake smile) Especially with a dead rat or bird. Anyway, dogs can learn tricks.

LESLIE: Dogs drool on their toys, which is gross, and some cats can learn tricks.

LAUREN: Whatever. Cats can't learn tricks.

LESLIE: Some cats can.

LAUREN: I doubt it.

LESLIE: Fine. Have you ever visited a friend and their dog won't just be quiet for a little while, while you talk to your friend? To make matters worse, they pee when they get excited. EW! Cats won't do that because they try to avoid people.

LAUREN: Your cat doesn't avoid people.

LESLIE: She does to strangers, but not to some of my friends.

LAUREN: I see now.

LESLIE: I can't think of anything else to say about this and I'm tired. We don't have a winner.

LAUREN: (smiles) Yes we do. Cats AND dogs are good pets for people, I think . . .

The End

Princess for Life

Mr. Banger persuasive essay number two! The title explains it. This is how my dad would handle an argument, so yeah, needless to say, I wouldn't win!

Reasons why Izzy Should or Shouldn't get a Part-time Job (2004)

IZZY: Do you believe that I'm totally responsible, Dad?

DAD: Well, you know that no one person is 100% responsible . . .

IZZY: True, but do you believe I'm close to what you'd call totally responsible?

DAD: Most of the time.

IZZY: But not all the time?

DAD: Right.

IZZY: So you believe I can, no, *should* grow to be more responsible?

DAD: (panics) Well, of course! But where are you going with this Izzy?

IZZY: Well, I *do* have a point, sir.

DAD: Sorry.

IZZY: Now, you're a very responsible man, Dad . . .

DAD: (flattered) Well, thank you. (grins)

IZZY: (rolls eyes) But, you got to be because of your job, right? What if you weren't responsible?

DAD: Well, *yeah*. If I wasn't, I'd get fired!

IZZY: So, are you saying a job helps make you more responsible? And if so, then a job would not only force me to be responsible at work, but also everywhere I go, right?

DAD: Yes, but you already have to have an amount of wisdom and *be* very responsible before you can be trusted with a job, which, sorry, but you are not there yet! And anyway, you should already be responsible to everyone and everywhere because I say so!

IZZY: (shocked and sighs) Okay, okay. I can buy that. But, sir, I know how you love to save money and if I got a job, then I would get money . . .

DAD: Well, that's usually how it goes . . .

IZZY: I would use that money to buy my own things.

DAD: (laughs) Oh, gosh! I know exactly what you would do. You would go out and buy CDs and video games and DVCs . . .

IZZY: It's DVDs

DAD: Whatever, those thingys, and then you'd come to me and say (in a baby voice) "Daddy! I need some money, please?" (normal voice) And give me those puppy eyes.

IZZY: Dad, I'm 17. I would not do that!

DAD: Oh yes you would!

IZZY: (stomps) WOULD NOT DADDY!

DAD: (grins) Okay, but will you (gets in Izzy's face) Buy your own food? Your own clothes? Your own home? WOULD YOU? WOULD YOU IZZY?

IZZY: (pale) N-N-No, no sir.

DAD: And why is that Izzy?

IZZY: Because the law states you have to provide for me until I'm 18 years of age.

DAD: (impressed) Well now, you do listen in school.

IZZY: (grins) Well, I do because I *am* responsible.

DAD: Maybe. But, why do you need a job when that same law says that I must provide for you? Not only food, but all your basic needs?

IZZY: Well, true, but CDs are not a basic need.

DAD: Then you don't need them.

IZZY: Yes I do.

DAD: Why? Will you die without them?

IZZY: Well, not really.

DAD: Then you don't need them, you . . .

IZZY: Want them?

DAD: There we go! Okay, now I understand.

IZZY: So, I can get a job?

DAD: (evil smile) Not yet.

IZZY: SHOOT!

DAD: (makes his hand shaped like a gun) POW! (laughs to himself) Any who, why do you want to buy these things on your own?

IZZY: To be independent.

DAD: Good answer. But, really, do you want to work instead of surfing the net? Do you really want to wear a uniform instead of what you choose? Do you really want to be around your friends all the time or mean strangers? Do you want to boss yourself around or be bossed around?

IZZY: No sir. I . . . I guess not.

DAD: If you want money, then go work . . .

IZZY: Like a job?

DAD: (laughs) NO! Like babysit and also save your allowance.

IZZY: If I can a job, I don't need one.

DAD: I can stop it right now.

IZZY: Never mind.

DAD: Thought so. But, really, do you want your school work to suffer? Because just because you have a job doesn't mean a teacher will go easy on you.

IZZY: Yeah. That wouldn't be fair.

DAD: Do you understand now?

IZZY: Crystal!

DAD: Should we go over all of it again?

IZZY: (freaks) NO, NO Dad, I got it! (runs away screaming)

The End

Smile; it burns
more caleries!

Okay! This is by FAR my favorite script before 2009 EVER! For my dad's history class (he was my teacher if you didn't know), we did a huge 1920s unit, including having to write a skit and present it, with props, clothes, and cramming as many '20s terms as possible. I got to do it with my best friends Marissa, Erin, and Kristen. I wrote the script and we practiced hard, even got costumes from my mom's clothing shop she had at the time. It was so much fun!

Being a flapper, I had to be "intoxicated," right? They had a camera set up for all the groups and my dad still has all of these. Well, Kristen, the bartender, brought in a real shot glass she had. We were in the middle of our skit, being all violent, and Marissa barely brushed the shot glass on our counter and it fell and shattered. We all stopped and stared, the audience quiet. Erin, the police officer, backed away and said, "It goes downhill from here." Boy, she was right! Because of the glass, all the fight scenes were so lame since we could not get on the floor, even though we planned them to sound cool from the side. At the end, my dad was trying not to smirk and our male classmates shook their heads at us and told my dad, "Too violent!" HA!

I figured since I was the innocent one of the group, IF I ever did get drunk (I have never taken more than a sip of alcohol ever; I don't like the taste or the burn, so me getting drunk is near impossible), I'd become this super angry, super strong chick! I'll let you figure out the rest for yourself, but enjoy the skit and decoding all the terms.

1920s Skirt (2004)

Setting: A speakeasy in 1920. Joe, the bartender, is cleaning the bar table. Camren and Lucy walk in, laughing

CAMREN: (snaps) Gin mill! Two shots of giggle water.

JOE: Copacetic. It cost a clam.

CAMREN looks in purse. It's empty. Gives LUCY a sad look.

LUCY: Looks like we spent our money at the other speakeasies downtown.

JOE: (crosses arm, firm) No money, no hair of the dog.

CAMREN: Rats! (snaps)

LUCY: (grabs Joe by the collar) Dry up you sap and give us some panther sweat now, jake?

JOE: (swallows hard) But . . .

LUCY punches JOE, who falls behind the counter and rises, holding his cheek a few seconds later.

LUCY: Now, what do you say?

JOE: Right away. (begins to pour drinks)

AARIN walks in and goes to talk to JOE. CAMREN and LUCY sit at the bar, waiting for their drinks.

CAMREN: Lucy, you got the hope chest?

LUCY: Sure do. (hands Camren a cigarette)

AARIN watches them, then talks to JOE.

AARIN: Joe, are these rummies giving you any trouble?

JOE: Yeah, I want them to mooch, but I think they're too bent to listen.

AARIN: True. They seem really fired!

JOE: So right!

AARIN: I'll tell them to leave.

AARIN walks over to LUCY and CAMREN.

CAMREN: (wiggles back and forth in chair) Oh look Lucy! A flat foot! Want a ciggy?

AARIN: No thanks. How many shots have you had tonight?

JOE: None here.

LUCY: (gives Joe an evil look) Not yet!

JOE: (scared, hands girls their drinks) Sorry.

LUCY: Finally! (takes a sip) Nifty!

CAMREN: (drinks some of hers) It's just ducky!

AARIN: I am sure it is, but how many shots have you had today?

CAMREN: Hmmmmm . . . Two, no wait, this many. (sways, holds seven fingers, then falls out of seat with a loopy smile on her face)

LUCY: What's it to you?

AARIN: Let's take you flappers downtown.

CAMREN: (jumps up from the floor, all excited) Are we going for a ride?

LUCY: (hits Camren in the head) NO you dumb Dora! Anyway, we're not done, so we're staying right here.

AARIN: You need to come with me.

CAMREN: (points at her) She said no!

AARIN: I think you need to.

JOE: Do what he says you birds.

LUCY: Dry you, you gin mill!

AARIN: Jake . . . That's it! Now!

CAMREN: We said no you fat flat-foot!

AARIN: FAT?! Stop acting screwy you saps! Jeepers Creepers! Come with me now.

LUCY: (says snarky and loud) Oh, go back to drinking your cup of Joe and dunking your little sinkers and leave us alone you lazy flat-foot!

CAMREN: (looks at Aarin's stomach) You are fat! (points to it) Do you have two stomachs or is it just five? (laughs hard and trips on own feet)

JOE: Oh, you girls better shut your kissers!

AARIN: (super mad, grabs nightstick) You ladies are under pinch right now, darn it!

CAMREN: Rats! We have been lousy tonight. Oh well! At least we get a jalopy ride! (grins and bounces up and down)

LUCY: You think you're hard-boiled, but all we want is some whoopee, away from our dapper!

CAMREN: (giggles) You're so evil!

AARIN: You're both totally blotto!

LUCY: That's an earful! (punches Aarin in the jaw)

AARIN: (comes up quickly, looking furious) All right, I'm getting the engagement rings out!

CAMREN: Oh, no, no, no! We're fine! (walks forward and trips. Aarin grabs her before she lands on the floor. Lucy punches Aarin again and grabs Camren)

AARIN: (punches Lucy's cheek) NOW!

LUCY rams AARIN to the floor and they fight on the left side of the stage.

JOE: She's a bearcat. That flat-foot needs to beat her good!

CAMREN: What did you say?

JOE: I said . . . (Camren punches Joe's face. Joe falls behind the counter. He gets up slowly) YOU . . . LET'S GO!

JOE and CAMREN fall behind the bar and fight for eight seconds with lots of noise. LUCY and CAMREN are the only two that emerge. They dust off and fix their hair.

LUCY: Well, that was the cat's meow!

CAMREN: Yeah. Tonight was too keen. We should rig the speakeasy. (trips)

LUCY: Let's ankle out of here! (loops her arm through Camren's as they walk away) Camren?

CAMREN: What's shaking Lucy?

LUCY: Remind me to never go to this speakeasy again. The service here is too slow.

The End

Short Stories

"I stir you, I smack you. I haunt you, I cling to you. I watch you, I ignore you. I smile at you, I glare at you. I think of you, I block you . . . What are these feelings called? I love you so much I hate you, or I hate you so much I love you?"

—Morgan Straughan Comnick

This was my first story for my creative writing class I took with Mr. Banger my sophomore year. It is based on an assignment I worked on for him that he never collected the previous year! HA! The original assignment was to write a short story about Margaret Sanger, the woman who was determined to help women learn about birth control. This story is shorter than the first draft, where the woman at the end tells her whole sad story. For length purposes, I cut that out before giving this to Mr. Banger, but the point and message is still there. This was written in late 2004.

The chilly winter breeze hit my face with full force, like a sharp blade. My eyes were blinded by the heavy layers of snow falling. As I exited the hospital, the rows of buildings shined in sparkling white glory. Even though the buildings looked lovely, I had to be careful. I had a long walk to the court house and the sidewalks were glazed over in slippery ice. I held onto the miles of buildings so I would not fall. I stopped, thinking of lying down for a brief moment, but then, I gazed up at her. Her, who was standing so proud and bold, yet had a forgiving and peaceful face looking over the glittering city. I smiled and walked on. Little did I realize that day would be the fateful day that set the course for the rest of my future.

I could not be late, not today. That brisk Friday was the last weekend I got to spend with my brother before he left to join the army. It took me awhile, but somehow, I managed to get to the court house on time and then, I saw him: a tall, handsome and strong young man with light brown hair in curls and sparkling, clear water eyes that reflected the light of the blinding sun. I ran into his opened arms and his affectionate smile. I was all warm inside now and also really happy to see him; my only family, my hero.

He gently kissed my forehead and said, "I was worried you would miss our big evening."

"OH, I would never! Not in a million years!" I yelled, jumping excitedly. He then grabbed my arm lightly and looped it through his own as we walked back to our home, away from the cold.

I walked in delicately, scared of damaging the perfect coziness of our cottage nestled in the heart of the city. I could already smell the sweet smell of pine that gently hit my face like a petite angel had just flapped her wings towards us as a reward for working. I could feel the warm glow from the rusty fireplace as the flames blazed high and the hot embers danced to the rhythm of my breath. Home always gave me such a wonderful feeling, almost as good as Christmas time does to an innocent child. I took off my coat and happily danced on the colored rug, like I always do to thank the Lord for my gift of life and this lovely small and tidy home. Then, a thought came to me . . . my brother was going to the army and I had no idea why.

While I was cooking supper, I kept trying to think of why. My deep concentration of the question my heart was yearning to answer made me almost burn the chili I was preparing and destroy the fine silver pot. Why was he leaving me? Maybe I said or did something to offend him that made my dear brother want to leave me or he was just sick of taking care of his kid sister. I should apologize, yet I was not sure that was the problem. Stressing myself out was only giving me a major headache. The more important question would be: Why was not I trying to stop him?

At the dinner table, the two of us talked about our days at work. I am a junior nurse and he is the co-owner of a newspaper stand downtown or, I should have said he *was*. I felt a pair of confused eyes stare at me; he must have noticed I did not pay attention to a word that came out of his mouth.

Softly, he asked me a question that startled me out of my state of darkness, "Margaret, my dear, would you like to talk?"

I slowly looked at him in fright, shaking hard to not allow him to know my pain. My chest was about to burst from the pressure as my vision blurred and his angelic face swirled in front of my scared eyes. Then, from out of nowhere, an unknown force from inside me exploded and I screamed at the top of my lungs, "WHY ARE YOU LEAVING ME AND TRYING TO GET KILLED?!" I gasped and quickly covered my mouth in horror. My eyes began to sting and rows of hot tears were rolling down my face in uncontrollable and painful amounts matching with its new red color.

Shocked, he looked at me for a moment, yet to my surprise, his eyes became forgiving, showing the good nature he has always had since we were small. My brother, focused and concerned with a smile approached me and laid his hands gently on my cheeks, staring into my spirit broken eyes. In his soft, kind, and deep voice, he said, "Margie, babe, you know I would never want to leave my baby sister since Mother and Father died. You mean the world to me . . ."

In fear of hurting me more and forming the right words, my guardian swallowed hard and then continued. "But, my duty belongs to my country and I know, that in my heart, I must do this. I feel that America will be in this war very soon—"

"Impossible!" I interrupted, upset by his disloyalty to our beloved nation. "Wilson promised that—"

"I know that our president is doing the best he can, but he cannot hold on for much longer, thanks to them bloody Germans! I just feel like I must go." My brother did have a sixth sense about awful situations, sadly enough for me.

"Brandon, I am seventeen! I am old enough to help. Let me go and be by your side! I . . . I just cannot stand the thought of us not being together," I said.

He stared deeply into my eyes, seeing right through me and into my hollow soul. "Never! Father would be extremely upset with us, with me, if I put you in harm's way; I would never forgive myself! I know you are old enough, but you know as well as I do, that women cannot join the army. The law is the law Margaret."

I stopped my tears, and nodded, saying that I understood his reasoning. Yet, I still felt horrid and all I could say to him was "I wish I could help America . . ." in a timid whisper.

He grinned big, giving me a boyish grin that relaxed my body in an instant. "You will. You have your own duty to America that you must uphold."

I smiled back and at the same moment, time allowed us to hold on to each other for one last supper together. However, not before we shared a heartfelt embrace; it was the worst hug of my life for it was the hardest to let go willingly.

Brandon and I spent a wonderful weekend in the main part of the Big Apple, shopping, viewing entertainment and laughing the whole way. Yet, before I knew it, the train came to take my brother away from me, possibly forever. There were numerous amounts of families saying good-byes to their brave young men that they loved more than themselves. Brandon kept kissing my forehead and cheeks repeatedly, making me giggle. No matter how difficult it was, I forced myself not to cry for his sake; I did not want him to worry and I wanted him to know I was proud of him more than I ever thought I could be.

"Be careful my dear. I will write you every day and be back soon."

My nerves got the best of me. "But what if you meet a beautiful British girl, marry her and forget all about me, your poor, lonely, annoying out of the blue little sister?!"

Blinking twice in an odd daze, he tried with all his might not to fail, but failed miserably. "Well, if that happens, I will tell her sorry because, if she wants me, she will have to come home and meet the other woman in my life, an unbelievably pretty and special girl." He winked. It made me blush a bright shade of red. It could happen though; he has always been extremely handsome and gentle-hearted.

Then, it happened: the final whistle. Something happened I did not expect. I lost control of my body as my heart, flooding with emotions, took over. I hugged him tight, not willing to let him go.

"I cannot breathe," he said, slowly turning blue and purple in the face. Feeling the same sorrow as I, he managed to give me one last, sweet kiss on the cheek, but he pushed me to the ground and ran towards the train like the wind. I was so shocked that I stayed on the ground in tears. I looked up to see him in the window and to my amazement, it appeared that he was crying as well. He gave me a quick wave with a somber look on his lips and hid his face from me. I ran after the train, but I realized it was pointless. My brother was gone and I was all alone.

"WHY, why would you do this to him? He just turned seventeen! He will surely die!" I turned around. At the corner of the station was a woman sobbing and a man right behind her, glaring at her in anger. "He is not strong, really shy and you knew he did not want to go, so why?!" She sounded angry; it made me feel angry too.

"He is a man! He is your oldest child . . ."

"Our oldest child!" she screamed, butting his harsh comment.

He went on. "I do not claim him! He was going to die soon, now let him die with honor." I could not believe what I was hearing! Who would want their child to die such a horrible way, no matter if it is good for the nation?! The woman laid on the ground, saying words through large tears that I could not make out; she was chanting the song in her heart that stabbed her spirit. Suddenly, the man's eyes then grew cold enough to kill a pack of bears.

The man grabbed his wife's arm, making a puffy ring around her wrist and slapped her hard across her right cheek of her sunken face! "DANG IT WOMAN! You better shut that mouth. That boy was weak! Not near good enough to carry my family name."

The broken woman shook her head. "You are . . . wrong! I only wanted six children at the most. You would not let me stop. You would beat me up, not caring if our children died. You even beat them up for no reason at times and killed one of our little girls! You never loved me, did you?! You only wanted to show off those children and me, for us to work for you, is that right?!"

He only looked down at her. "Women have no say," he whispered so evilly that the woman almost fell backwards; she quickly caught herself, scared she would fall into the underworld for he must have been working for Satan. "Now, I am going to the bar to play poker. You best have dinner ready or else . . ."

She slowly stood, holding her delicate cheek. Blood slipped through her fingers, showing the world the scars she had suffered. My heart sank; that had to be the worst day of my life!

I was about ready to leave when I noticed a letter was stuck to the heel of my foot. It had my name on it, or at least my last name and address! I opened it up and it read:

Dear fellow American,

We are pleased to inform you that your loved one has the bravery and skills to be one of the selected few to join our first test army to go "over there" with General Perishing. President Wilson wishes you and your family the best of luck. Our boys will be home soon.

From: United States of America Army Board

I dropped the paper in disbelief. Brandon was right; Wilson broke his promise. America was broken and now a lost cause like Europe . . .

No, Wilson had not broken America; he had only wounded it. I kept thinking back to that woman. Her story was so common at our hospital, yet there was a way to fix it . . . called birth control. For some reason, no one knows about it and nurses are not allowed to advertise it. This information must be relayed to that needy woman, to every woman. We can save lives and cost this way if only . . . I paused . . . is this my duty that I must uphold to America, like Brandon said? I am not sure, but for the first time, I felt hopeful and all right to be alone without my brother at my side. This warmth coming from my chest was so welcoming, like I had my family with me again. No matter what the outcome could be, I wanted this feeling to last.

I stood there, staring at her again. Her smile seemed different that day; it looked like it was just for me, saying, "You can do it . . ." I waved back to her, the lovely Statue of Liberty. Slowly, I walked out of the train station. America will be on the rocks for a while, but I was willing to try my hardest to uphold my duty for this country, like my brother. God speed my love to him. I am Margaret Sanger, and someday, the world will know about birth control. This is my oath.

Short Story for Mr. Banger number 2. Our only requirement for this assignment was we had to use the name Amaranth for one of the characters. I cannot recall why, but this is what I wrote. I had to change the ending though because Mr. Banger said it was *too* dark and unrealistic! HA! This was written in late 2004.

She looked innocent enough as she slept on the love seat of her parents' screened porch. Curled up like a roly poly, her stringy hair hung nearly to the worn, wooden floor below. The late morning sun projected a strange mural on the wall behind the love seat. Inside, Amaranth's parents knew their daughter had experienced a rough night, but they also knew she would be belligerent if awakened prematurely.

As they huddled at the kitchen window, Amaranth suddenly rotated the pillow 180 degrees and was comforted by the fresh coolness of the other side. Slowly, a delicate dragonfly buzzed happily around the lily of the valleys potted on the porch rail. The sun beat down upon the dragonfly. He decided to rest on top of Amaranth's smooth nose. Quickly, the angle hidden with its wings, the dragonfly flew in the front yard meadow, revealing a small, shy, and beautiful young child with huge, sparkling blue eyes. The young girl stared at Amaranth, her soft skin glowing and her face so pure, the expression almost heartbreaking.

Amaranth awoke and looked into the girl's pools with sorrow and anger. "Sakura? What's the matter?"

Sakura looked at her hero like she had just crushed her dreams into the ground, washed away her hopes, and ruined her life.

"Sister . . ." Sakura stared.

Amaranth's mood changed in a snap. Her pale, sky eyes burned with fire. She showed her teeth like a mad dog, reading to attack for its kill. Her hands trembled like an earthquake full of fear and panic. Pain too.

"You *cannot* call me that!" Amaranth screamed.

She turned her head away in complete shame for her action. Shadows showed her tears, shining like prism lights.

In a dry, dark voice, she whispered to Sakura between tears, "I am adopted! I have always been, but I only found out last night. Since, now, my sister is twenty-one and can take full rights for me now by law . . ."

She had to breathe, calm her thoughts, let them have an even pace so she would not scare Sakura, the most darling gift God could have given her . . . if they were related that is.

Sakura held her hands together, shivering in the sunset. Her expression was frozen in stone. Time had locked her in a nightmare of reality. Her chestnut hair blew elegantly in the breeze.

Amaranth slowly walked up to Sakura, smiling at her with her best poker face. Tears began to drop on Amaranth's hand, which was resting gently on Sakura's cheek.

"Oh my Sakura! I love you more than life itself. It's been hard work. Cooking, cleaning, gardening . . . Lord, planting all those stupid flowers!" She laughed to herself. "But, you guys are too wonderful. I'll be so sad to leave you. I'm so sorry sweetheart."

Sakura rammed into her sister's chest with open arms, ramming it hard. They embraced each other tightly. Nothing could tear them apart at this moment but their own will.

* * *

That night after dinner, Amaranth lay in her bed thinking of how her life was a lie, a wonderful dream that only seemed real. The moonlight hit Amaranth's hair, which was flying every which way on the bed cover. The moon showed the desire and loneliness of a young girl's face, something the moon never wanted to see. It slowly faded behind the trees, hiding from Amaranth's scared face.

"We'll say she moved away, ran away. I'll say anything to get my daughter back!"

Amaranth quickly sat up like a princess, hearing the anger in her lovely mother's voice. Mrs. Morning-Glory's voice went on.

"How can you not say anything Touya! She's our daughter. I'll stop them anyway I can!" she yelled. She was talking to Mr. Morning-Glory, a kindhearted man, like she hoped her real father was.

Mrs. Morning-Glory cleared her throat and said in the lowest voice ever reached. "How would you feel if someone took Sakura away from you?" Mrs. Morning-Glory's eyes snapped in anger.

"That's no different! I won't let them take Amaranth! Never! I love her too much! We raised her!" She suddenly went into sobbing.

"I love her too Nadishiko, but . . . she's not our daughter," he whispered. "Not by law anyway . . ."

Amaranth's heart sank and then broke into a million and one pieces. She didn't want to leave, but she had always wondered why she wasn't as happy-go-lucky as the Morning-Glories. What should she do?

"Stop this Touya! You jerk!" Mrs. Morning-Glory screamed.

Amaranth fell back on her bed, tears building up in her eyes. She had never, in her whole life, heard the Morning-Glories fight. They were the perfect couple, the perfect good-hearted family. She had ruined them. She had torn them apart from true happiness, which they more than earned.

They were yelling back and forth, making the walls feel depressed. She couldn't take this heck she felt inside her heart! She threw the pillow with all her might at the door and yelled as loud as she could, "SHUT UP! JUST SHUT UP! I HATE YOU GUYS! So, please, just shut up!"

Amaranth began to cry again, hard. She couldn't stop. It grew silent in the hallway, not one word was heard, no sound, but Amaranth's crying.

"I love you," she finally choked through her tears. The rest of the night, she cried and cuddled her knees as she rocked herself to a rough sleep.

* * *

Amaranth spent all of the next morning sitting on the front porch, looking at her old world, waiting for her sister to come. She was picking her up today, so they could live together now, forever. Sakura sat with her, looking out at the world, acting grown-up until she saw a butterfly play in the grass of the front yard. She chased it in good, harmless fun. Amaranth had to smile shyly, watching her baby sister be normal. She rested her head on her pinned skirt.

Sakura stopped playing for a short moment and went to her sister's side. Brightly showing her pretty teeth, she forced her sister to look, but went into a slump herself as her sister was not smiling. Sakura quickly sat down and copied Amaranth's motion exactly. Again, Amaranth showed no life in her gestures.

Sakura looked at Amaranth and in a baby voice, asked, "So, what's your new sister like?"

Amaranth slowly looked at her in shock, her eyes hurt. She changed her sad glance to look at the grass below her cold feet.

"Well," Amaranth began, "I have no idea about her really. All I know is that she is twenty-one, lives in a small apartment in the city, and she's training to be a publisher."

Sakura laughed, "That's funny. She seems like a city slicker . . . You're a city slicker too then."

Amaranth put Sakura in a headlock and laughed with her.

"Yeah, I guess she is. But, not me. Never me! My parents were simple city folk. Like ours . . . yours, without so much country style. I don't remember anything really. I was two when they died in a car crash. I bet my mom was kindhearted and lovely . . ."

Sakura jumped up, "Like you Amaranth!"

Amaranth laughed, "No way!" She grabbed her knees and rocked back and forth. "And my old man was funny too I am told. I do have the weirdest laugh! I wonder if we could have been a loving family if the accident hadn't torn us apart?"

The only sound made was the melody of the early grasshoppers. Then, a car pulled up.

Finally, the burning lights that Amaranth never wanted to walk into came for her. A yellow taxi pulled in the driveway to pick her up to meet her sister at the airport. The license plate read DEAD66, which was strange. Amaranth quickly rubbed it off though as she grabbed her suitcase, which was resting on the painted porch. Sakura had the saddest look in her eyes as she slowly walked Amaranth to the cab.

"Amaranth! Amaranth dear!" It was Mrs. Morning-Glory, screaming and running straight for the girls. She ran very fast for the loving yet large woman! Her kind eyes met the two curious young land angels. As she caught her breath, she began to speak in a sorry voice.

"Deary, I got a call from your lawyer's office. You sister was in a car crash honey . . . Your sister's in a coma . . ." She hung her head and made a cross over her chest.

Sakura and Amaranth looked at each other in silence for a short moment. Amaranth's knees buckled underneath her, her suitcase flying behind her. Her mind could not even process how to react.

Sakura spun around between her mother and sister and then threw her arms on Amaranth's back. A breeze blew a mini storm around her kimono robe. She smiled kindly at her older sister. "Well, until they figure this out, you always have a home with us."

Amaranth stopped, gazing at the amazing sun which was shining its full and way rays towards them. A cloudless sky showed a dove flying toward that sun. Amaranth gave Sakura a shy smile, tapping her little cheek, making the young girl blush. Gently, Sakura jumped down and grabbed her mom's hand as she stared at her hero with light once more.

Amaranth gave a fullest of glory smile to the world, her long hair flowing.

"Dear God, please heal and protect my sister." She began, talking to the smiling sky. "But Lord, I think this is the best life I can lead."

My third assignment for creative writing for Mr. Banger. This one required we use the sentence as our first sentence. This one gets sort of dark and in an area of thirteen plus. I honestly am shocked I wrote the ending the way I did, but I think it is right. I wanted to use all of Lisa and Annie's siblings in a full story, but it never happened. Read on! Fall 2004.

Her doctor said the infection would go away in a few days. A sharp pain of relief came right inside of me. I could actually breathe now and ask the question I had locked up inside me.

"Please tell me, sir. What's wrong with her?

The doctor's eyes became kind, but his voice was very business-like, "Miss, all she has are some bumps that can only be caused sexually. She'll be in pain for a little while, but I promise, when the bumps go away, so will the pain."

A feeling of anger raged inside my body. I started to shake, but all I could do was say, "Only sexually? How could this happen?"

He only stared at me coldly and said, "She must tell you that!"

He gave me such an evil look that it made me fall back into the waiting room chair. I was so scared now. If these "bumps" did not kill her, my father surely would.

Three years ago, my father shot my eldest brother James because he stood up for me when my father was slapping my face for no reason. I swear, his veins are full of ice and his heart is made out of only steel. Tears flew down my face, thinking of what he would do to my sister.

Then, I heard a squeak. I jumped, thinking it was the Grim Reaper, ready to take my sister to the place she did not belong. But, it was not. There, slowly walking out the wooden doorframe of the hospital office was Lisa, as pale as a spirit, looking almost dead. Her eyes were as big as a moonlight owl's, staring at you with only the focus of fear. She was staring at me now, looking at me like she had never seen me before. Now, the wall became her main focus and her eyes were full of horror.

"Lisa?" I whispered. She didn't move. She only became paler.

"Lisa?!" I yelled. Again, nothing.

"Lisa, *please!*" I screamed. She didn't try to move. I fell to the floor in tears, crying my eyes out. Why have you done this to her God?

"An . . . Annie?" She got out the weakest whisper possible.

I stopped crying. Only tears of joy ran down my face. I looked up, staring at her like an angel. "Ye . . . Yes?" I said to her.

Without moving, she asked me, "I am going to live, right?"

I felt that sharp pain of relief again. I grinned at her and said, "God will be with you . . ."

She smiled a little and fell to the floor next to me, stretching on the small, leaf green carpet of the waiting room. She then wiped away the tears on my cheeks and put her hands in mine, saying with a smile, "As long as you believe in me, I will try my best."

I then remembered I had to ask her what happened. She couldn't have gotten those bumps alone! I decided now was not the best time. She needs rest. And besides . . . I have no idea what I am going to ask.

Lisa and I slowly walked home together. It was a nice November day, crisp for a midmorning. The leaves were mostly gone or hiding in the grasses, but the ones still hanging on were so lovely, the oranges, yellows, browns, and reds all so elegant. It was cold of course, with a strange on and off breeze hitting our faces, but I felt perfect in my church coat Mama made for me, though Lisa was shaking to the cold. I had to walk faster. It was strange that there were no birds, no animals out at all. And the sky was so gray, spoiling the Earth's beauty. Is this a sign from God? I bet it is! We better get home, get home before he does.

I tiptoed to the gate of our home and slowly opened the backdoor that led to the kitchen. As I opened the door, the wonderful smell of bread baking filled the air. Mother was by the stove, stirring the stew. I gently kicked my book against the door so she could hear me. It worked like a charm! She quickly let us come in as I rushed Lisa to my room in the attic (Susan was in her room) before Father saw us. Lisa did not like this, but she did as I told her. She needed rest.

I went downstairs to help Mama with dinner. Anything to get Lisa's pain off my mind. Mother stared at me oddly after she tied her apron. I knew what she wanted to know by her look. So, I thought I better answer her.

"She will be all right. She has to rest for a while. The poor thing wore herself out!"

Mother made a cross over her chest and whispered, "Thank the good Lord's name!"

"Annie! You're back!" I was about to peel potatoes when Megan screamed at me and jumped into my arms, or tried to! I fell to the floor and we were giggling. Mother only stood there and smiled. I got up and told her to hush. She laughed again and ran to get our other siblings: Fred, Carmel, Sally, and Susan. They all stood in the doorway of the living room and kitchen.

Susan grabbed little Fred in her arms, making her look mature and lovely. She had very long, very dark, very wavy hair, gorgeous honey brown eyes, and the most elegant tanned skin. She was not real tall, but was the sweetest of angels. Everyone says we look like twins. True, we have the same long hair, but mine is lighter and only wavy at the ends. I have ocean blue eyes and peachy-colored skin. I am taller than her, but I should be; I *am* one year older than her! She will be a great mother one day. She could be now if she liked. She is fifteen.

Sally was nine and looked exactly like Mama. A little pug nose, sky blue eyes, baby doll like skin. Her long hair was a pure gold color and so shiny. She even has Mama's loving smile.

Carmel is the cutest little thing in the world! Her long hair is the exact same color as caramel. Her eyes are hazel white, like an angel's, and her little skin is a normal white, but with a pinch of a brown sugar tan. She is so sweet for seven.

Cannot forget my baby brother Fred. He is so adorable for two! Blond, almost white hair, navy eyes, and soft, baby skin along with the cutest rosy cheeks. He had Lisa's cute laugh.

Megan (who is ten), ran to all her siblings to join the perfect family portrait. Her long brown hair stayed perfectly straight, like it always did. Her blue eyes and pale skin had her simple features stand out, but she was still pretty.

Sally finally asked what everyone else was thinking, "How's Lisa, Annie?"

Mother answered the question before I could open my mouth, "She will be fine honey. We all have to let her rest for a while, all right?" She winked.

"Of course!" Carmel jumped up happily. "I will do all her chores!"

Susan grabbed her shoulder and smiled, "No you will not; *we* all will. Anything for Lisa."

They all happily agreed. I stood in the corner, looking at my shadow in shame. What would they think if they knew the truth? I did not even know the truth! I had to find out fast before it gets out of hand. I decided to ask Lisa when I brought her supper to her later.

I opened the door to the attic to see Lisa sitting up on the bed, half asleep. Her long, stringy blonde hair looked oily and was hanging everywhere on my pillow. Her skinny self could barely support her boney body. She closed her book when she saw me and smiled big at me and the tray of her favorite foods. I acted shy around her all of a sudden.

"Are you hungry?"

She nodded. I gently placed the tray on her lap. She grabbed her spoon and loudly took a sip of her stew and happily nodded, meaning it was good I guess. Something came out of me. I wanted to ask her if she was crazy for making herself get those bumps. Instead, this came out: "Are you mad . . ." I stopped. She looked at me with such a disappointed face. I had to catch myself and change the question, " . . . at me?" Yeah. Are you mad at me?" I yelled this in her face.

She blinked a couple of times and giggled like Fred. "Oh Annie. I never would be, never could be. I stopped talking because I know it bothers you. You worry too much!" Usually, when she does this, I tickle her, but I do not think she understands how awful this could be, what it could lead to, how awful I feel. I pray it is not what my nightmares wish it could become.

I quickly left the room. If only God could shoot me with lightning right now. I felt like I was letting my sister die, but I cannot accuse her of anything either. What will I do?

* * *

It has been three long weeks since Lisa's been sick and it has not been easy to hide her illness from Father. But, by some miracle, we were able to do it! Lisa kept saying she was doing fine enough to work, that she was getting better, but I could tell by her skin becoming pure white that she was not. Her eyes were almost pitch black and her hair was falling out a lot worse than usual. Something was wrong, really wrong, and I had to help. But, Lisa would not let me get near her and once, she snuck out in the middle of the night. This was making me nervous.

I wanted to ask her now and I had to ask her now! It has been a month since she became ill. I came home after school and threw my books on the floor, running upstairs as fast as I could. I met Mama in the middle of the stairs. She had tears in her eyes and her mouth was wide-opened and dry.

I looked at her and all she lipped with her mouth was "Dead."

I fell on the stairs and cried my head off almost. Lisa was dead! My heart felt like it was about to explode with anger and my eyes would float away with my tears. Why was I so scared? It was my fault. I was scared to ask my own blood a question of safety.

* * *

Dr. Stab invited me to his house after Lisa's funeral. He was the one who told me of her illness. But, why did the bumps not go away when she rested? We took good care of her, but . . . Did she work when she left that one night? Or, was it someone? Like, Father? All these thoughts made my mind spin with full force. I had to rest and realize what this man wants.

"I'm very sorry about your sister. Lisa was a beautiful young woman for eighteen. She had a wonderful future, but she was too weak," he said, like he knew everything about her. What did this man know?

All I could do was nod and say to his face, "Yes . . . She . . . She was grand . . ."

He slowly led me to the doorframe, out of his red rose living room, holding on to the back of my hand with one of his cold, mysterious ones. I felt so fooled, so small, so unimportant. I was finally able to get to the door, the night stars shining in a strange red light, yet still as lovely as ever. He spun me toward his face while I was about to walk out the door. I stared into his strange eyes, sparkling in the moonlight. I felt like I was floating, yet I was still small and worthless. He grabbed a piece of my hair and twisted it with his hairy finger.

"You are a very beautiful young lady, Miss Annie, for sixteen..." He whispered so softly in my ear, "You are almost as beautiful as your sister was . . ."

"What do you mean by that?" I demanded, still in his strong, almost painful embrace. Then, I had an awful feeling that I knew was right.

"You are the one? You are the one that did this to Lisa, were you not? You're the one that made her ill. It was all you! That is why you knew the bumps came so quickly! How could you do this? You are a Christian man!" I screamed, trying to jerk out of his hold on me, but he grabbed me tighter.

His smile became one with the Devil's. He laughed, "She did not disagree hardly once I convinced her after her birthday party, her entry into womanhood, how special I could make her. I think, she enjoyed it and she was good. Her home life was awful and I wanted to make her last bits of life fun for her. Her father would have surely killed her soon enough."

I kicked him as hard in the hurtful spot between his legs and ran out of his embrace. "I hope you burn for your misdeed!" I cried and I ran out into the snow-covered street. My eyes full of tears, I couldn't see at all. I tripped on ice on the ground, unable to move. A light came closer to me and all I heard was the sound of my unhappiness and a honk. I could have tried to move, but it was too late . . .

CRASH!

I could hear, but not very well. Speaking was impossible. I heard one person's voice and although I could not see or feel anything, I knew someone was lifting me up and staring at me.

"I am sorry Annie. I am sorry Lisa died. I am sorry. I knew she went to the doctor, but I did not stop her. I knew she was sick. I knew she would die honey. I wanted to end her pain, but I knew you could not handle it like when I had to shoot your brother. Your brother was so sick as well, like Lisa. He hid it from you Annie because he loved you so. I could not let my son suffer like that and when he asked me to do it . . . It was the hardest choice of my life. I had no idea you saw us! I care for all of you children. Do not worry Annie. I am sorry I let this happen to you. I hate to think I am losing another child . . ." The voice caught and I felt tears on my cheeks, "But, you will go to Heaven and he will not. Dr. Stab is dead. I got him good. I showed him what happens when he hurts my daughters."

Father . . . ? I knew it was him. I only felt a tear drop and a peck on my forehead. I used my last bit of energy to smile at him. I knew he loved me. He did not kill my brother for hatred and he had to act heartless ever since I saw him to keep my brother's secret. And the doctor is now where he belongs. He cannot hurt anyone else.

I took a long, hard breath. I was ready now to leave and go towards the light that was getting brighter, coming towards me. Inside the sun ball was Lisa and James, extending their hands to me. I was not scared any more. I reached towards them. I had found my cure for sorrow.

This is an anime inspired short story, once again, one I composed in Mr. Banger's creative writing class yet again in the fall of 2004. I was starting to get into *InuYasha* that year, so that is why many of my stories from this period in my life have more of a dark feel. This one takes place in the Feudal era of Japan with magic. I hope you sense the anime vibes . . . Please enjoy!

Her eyes were as gray as can be. Her lips so dry and weak and her long, once elegant hair was a huge mess of knots. Her skin was as pale as snow and shaking like she was in the middle of a storm. The whole world seemed to be in darkness . . . My whole world. The only thing I could see was a lavender sky, making deadly patterns in the dark. Her little hand lay into my palm, so helpless she was, my darling daughter. She cannot die, yet, she must . . .

As I stare at her, flashbacks zoom quickly before my eyes. I see her, the only woman I would ever love, standing under a cherry blossom tree, by a lake, her black and ivory hair moving in my direction. She smiled and I knew I always would want her. But, Kiku could not marry. It was against the law for a priestess like her. We tried to do everything to be together and there was only one way . . . have a child. Kiku did not want this. She said if that happened, she would never live it down. I had to do the only thing I could . . . make her by force!

I am not a bad person, but I was not going to be apart from her! Nine months later, my darling Aino was born, a wonderful name we gave her meaning "child of love" in our country of lovely Japan. I fell immediately in love again with this sweet child that was *mine*. Sadly, Kiku was only nice to her until she was almost three. She said that since I forced her to be a mother that once Aino was old enough, she would stop caring for her completely.

Even if Kiku said she did not love Aino (which was true by the way she treated her), Aino was the sweetest, prettiest, and happiest girl in the world. I loved her with all my heart. Her favorite thing to do was make up stories or gaze at the stars, making wishes. She always wished for little things, like pretty flowers to grow on her favorite hill or to find her prince charming. But, what she asked for most of all was for her mother to love her as much as she loved her. I would hear her cry at night at times, asking for Kiku . . .

Five months after Aino turned three and Kiku left, Kiku was trying to drag wounded soldiers off the battlefield to take them to camp to heal them. She was hit and killed on the field. I was heartbroken. Even though she was mean to us, I still and will always love her. Aino never got over this; she never stopped crying for her on her favorite hill.

By age four, Aino started to realize she had the power to read people's hearts and she could turn any flower into a spear when she snapped. Aino was extremely gentle with her training. I felt badly that I had to become a thief to get food for my own flesh and blood while she practiced.

Recent events enter my mind now. It happened yesterday. Aino had gotten ill a few days earlier. I was coming back from a steal when I heard her scream loudly. I ran from the river as fast as I could. Aino was running out of our cave, with flower spears all around her. In the dark stood . . . Kiku . . . Her ghost? Yet, she had her bow and arrows in her hands, aiming right at our Aino! She was trying to kill her own daughter!

All Aino could do was stare and cry, "Mommy! Please stop. Why do you hate me so?!"

I was in shock. She never died . . . She ran away from us, from Aino . . . from me.

She grinned evilly and laughed, "Well, you are still alive, Omega the thief? Surprised to see me alive, are you?"

I stepped closer to her, still in fear. I was about to touch her cheek when Aino yelled, "Daddy! Please stop! She's in love with another man! Her heart has no place for either of us in it. I can feel it easily! Please trust me!"

I stopped and had to ask, "You . . . You love . . . someone else . . . ?"

She grinned again and patted Aino's head, "My, my, my! Are you not smart? Yes, I met the real man of my dreams. He is handsome, tough, and a much better fighter than you Omega. But, if he dared found out I had a child, he would never stay with me. So, I have to kill her. I have always wanted to kill the thing I hate most anyway . . ."

Aino fell to the ground in tears and fainted. She was too weak from being ill. She may . . . She may . . . NO!

Kiku smirked and aimed at her target. I dived in front of her intention and grabbed Aino in my arms before the arrow got either of us. My former wife groaned, angrier, and got ready for another attack. We ran far and hard and finally lost her in the Dragon-Demon cave. Aino was much worse and if I did not hurry, she would die. But, if I did leave, Kiku may find her and kill her . . . What to do?

After my numerous flashbacks, I heard the sweetest little voice of a five year old, "Dad . . . daddy?"

I smiled down at her, "Yes sugar?"

She got the courage to talk, "Why . . . Why does mom . . . hate . . . me? I am so . . . sad . . . knowing I am . . . not loved . . ."

I gasped. She knew I was having a hard time on what to do. She was trying to help me choose. I cried in my hand. My other hand hit a soft part of the cave. Under the soil was a rose. It looked thousands of years old, yet it was almost perfect. My hand had yellow dust on it . . . star dust! It kept the rose alive. It gave me an idea.

I remember a spell I learned with star dust. It can turn you into a seed and when love hits it, the seed will be reborn with some memories, a chance to restart life. I asked Aino if she could handle this. She cried slowly, then nodded and looked at the night sky. A shooting star was coming our way, the best for wishing. She turned to kiss my cheek, smiling gigantically.

"It is for the best. As long as one day, we will meet and be together again."

I hugged her tight. That is what she must have wished for and it came true.

I chanted the magic words and closing her eyes, Aino became a lovely seed and her bright light went into my hands. I grinned and quickly ran out of the cave. I had to hide it, where I could find it, but Kiku never could. I then remembered a pretty forest . . .

It began to pour. There, in front of the forest was a man with long white hair, in a red warrior robe, a sword on his hip. I fell in the mud and looked into his cold, honey eyes. He threw me on my back and showed me a well deep in the forest where I could hide Aino. He said to me, "Only the true lover of two worlds could get in the well . . . and Kiku is not it."

I thanked him and gently laid the seed down.

As I slowly walked away, wanting to know how he knew Kiku, or could sense my spell, I had to ask him one thing, "Why help me?"

He stared coldly, "Because," he yelled, "This was all my fault . . . and I feel that one day, that little girl will be great use to Japan."

That made me happier. Aino would forget about me a little, but she would rebirth to love, make friends, and become a strong, beautiful young woman. Thanks to this stranger. We will find each other again. The star promised us so.

My first essay for my advance senior communication arts class and our only creative one! We had all these college bound rules to follow, like not using "and" at all and no contractions. The no contractions one has been instilled in me and I use it a lot, but the not using "and" rule . . . I only used it in this and another writing class my senior year in college. It is TOUGH!

Still, this story is dear to me. It is my retelling of how I met Derrick. I changed the names, but everyone knew who it was! Hehehe! One of the guys who had choir with him had to edit it for me in class. When reading my description of the male character, he looked sick and said, "Well. I never thought of Derrick that way . . ." HA! Also, notice the names Drew, Carmen, and Lucy (who are based off my pals Marissa, Jessica, and me). If anyone gets this trio reference, they get ten bonus points! ☺ This was written in Fall 2006.

I wish I wrote more creative stories in high school, but alas: mostly essays and college papers!

Pretending to show interest, I nodded delicately to Mrs. Stroud's ever growing chatter. It was the speech I have heard a hundred times over and had vivid nightmares about when I had trouble sleeping. There was nothing wrong with her words when in fact, they were quite beautiful, but the concept would never relate to me for I never thought I would ever be considered pretty by my peers of the opposite sex. Being a romantic at heart and having no one to express it towards was a drag, yet I accepted my fate, or what I thought to be my destiny. Snapping out of my bored daze from my sudden realization of hope, I laughed at myself lightly to notice that I had drawn a heart on my desk. Mrs. Stroud's final words were cut off by the bell's piercing wail. Not inspired by the so called "how to boost your self-esteem" speech, I steadily left the room to meet up with my pals; an ugly duckling mixed in a world of swans.

Sliding my feet to the rhythm of the school's movements, I walked to my last hour class with my fellow companions Drew and Carmen, all of us giggling without a care in the world it seemed.

Drew suddenly exploded with the excitement she tried to contain. "Rich is the best boyfriend ever guys! He loves all the bands I do; most people do not even know half of them. It really is perfect!"

Carmen raised her hand to add her own comment. "I know what you mean," she sighed in a romantic, breathy way, "Hill always wraps his arm around my waist when we sit together at lunch . . . What a dreamboat he is."

I shyly smiled at my two dearest friends. I loved them more than the earth loves the warmth from the sun, but I could not relate to their conversation. I helped both of them realize that "going out" with those guys would make them forever happy, but I could not do that for myself. I was the listener, the shoulder to cry on, and the planner. For once, I wished I could have at least one of those favors returned, but I suppose that would be selfish.

"Lucy, have you found anyone that meets your fancy yet?" Carmen interrupted my thoughts with her witty question she said with a rude smile. Her old fashion saying was added to make fun of the way I talk that I inherited from my father. To show her I was in dismay, I stuck my tongue towards her before answering.

"Well, not really." I brushed a loose hair from my eyes to cover the fact I was lightly blushing, "I really do not think there is anyone who would be attracted to me."

"That is not true at all Lucy!" Carmen said in shock, but still in a bubbly tone.

Thinking deeply, Drew placed her index figure under her chin. "I am not sure. If I could get a boyfriend before Lucy, who is cuter than me . . . Well, maybe something is wrong with you, girl, since the rest of the gang has someone, all fourteen of us . . ."

Hurt by her harsh comment, I blew the slap off from my face. To hide the doubts of my inner self, I replied jokingly while glaring, "Ha, ha Drew! I love you too!"

She beamed brightly, but Carmen covered her mouth before she could talk again. "So Lucy, did you not tell me that Oliver was trying to set you up with his best friend?"

The thought had actually left my mind for a moment. It was true; my good friend Oliver was trying to hook me up with his best friend. I have never seen the boy and all I knew was what Oliver had told me about him after school for the past two months, which I was not sure if they were true facts. Usually I refuse when my friends try to "hook me up" with a guy they know; it either ends in disaster or heartache for one of the two. Yet, the way he presented this one boy made me curious; I really did want to meet him since I found out he sings, the one joy I have in high school.

Tired of being silenced, Drew bit the top of Carmen's hand, making her scream a loud and hilarious wail. I chuckled in roaring laughter, not able to get enough breath into my lungs to ask Carmen if she was all right. Before I could stand up straight, Drew bumped Carmen out of the way and looked directly into my face, smiling. "Well, if this mystery geek does not work, I know a guy . . ."

I gave her the "talk to the hand" signal to tell her to cease. "No thank you. I have followed the thoughtful suggestions of my friends before and it has got me nowhere. Sorry, but never again."

Drew shrugged as Carmen began to yell at her for the bite and the two playfully argued until we went our separate ways for the hour. Pacing myself, I continued my journey on to class, thinking of what my friends had told me. Maybe I had no appeal to boys, but it never bothered me before, or at least, I never let it show. A thick fog filled my lungs as the air became heavy from the pain I was feeling inside. I guess I should not have let it affect me that I did not have a boyfriend. I had the rest of my life to set a course for it, but for some unknown reason, it did hurt, and awful badly too. The feeling of not being loved ate away at my soul. Time was at a standstill for me and before my dim eyes could focus on class, the five-minute dismal bell rang.

After the final bell, I set my quest to the lobby to wait for my father. There, I saw Oliver leaning on the brick post with his usual goofy smile. Spotting me almost instantly after I entered, he ran to me, picked me up like I was his bride and rushed me over to the bench near where he just was, startling me half to death. He plopped down next to me with a softcover yearbook in his hands from the previous year.

"Look up Lance Conwell in the sophomores section. I want you to see what he looks like." He winked after handing me the colorful book. Doing as told, I flipped quickly through the pages, creating a little breeze to cool myself down after my rushed kidnapping. Searching after some time, I noticed the name pop out "Lance Conwell." My index finger slid over to the fourth photo in the sixth row to see him, the mysterious best friend of Oliver. Staring at the photo, I captured a boy of true innocence, a lovely shaped body, a cheerful smile and a gentle nature. How I knew this, I was not sure, but I felt in my heart it was right. My chest became tight, like a hand was gently squeezing it and my eyes were locked on to his; I felt I was trapped under a spell.

I turned to talk to Oliver though my mouth went dry when I noticed he was gone like the wind. Confused, I began to pack up my things while holding that page of the book to my warm chest. While checking for my homework, I noticed my small pocket was opened. Alarmed, I looked to see inside; everything was there. Then, I felt the top of a plastic bag to feel it had been unzipped. I counted the items it contained to realize why the pocket was open; one of my wallet school pictures was missing. This mystery made me ponder until the darkest hour of the chilly night. All I could do was wait for sleep to come, but it was not meant to be for on that night, it had become my bitter enemy.

A brisk morning had passed before I got my head out of the clouds, imagining the boy's perfect form. I liked the way his name sounded after it left my tongue: Lance Conwell; so elegant and mysterious. All I could do was stare at his picture for an uncountable number of times at his face, making my heart race in fear; I was in love with a boy I have never met.

Before I could snap out my "puppy love" daze, it was homeroom. To help ease my mind from this entire new calamity, Mrs. Stroud sent me on a mission to turn in the tutoring forms for my classmates. It was a relief to breathe in the crisp air of the cafeteria and inhaled some interesting aromas by mistake. I was almost out the door to the next wing when a friendly and familiar voice reached my ears.

"Lucy! Come over here!"

Smiling from ear to ear, I noticed Oliver was waving at me like a mad man on fire with a large grin on his round face. Then, he signaled for me to hug him. I did as instructed and quickly walked to his table of guys, giving him a big hug.

"Hey Mrs. Conwell. How are you?" Oliver winked playfully. His comment made all the boys look up at me in astonishment as I shook in fear. I could feel the color of the reddest apple creep to my cheeks at lightning speed. My body was shaking like the devil had filled my veins with pure Arctic ice to tease me. My head pounded in the same fast tempo that my stressed-out heart was hammering. With my eyes stinging and vision blurry, I realized nothing could have been more humiliating. Yet, I was wrong. I was about to yell at him when I spotted a boy across the table. To my total surprise, it was not just any guy, but Lance himself!

Looking at his priceless face, my heart began to explode out of my chest. My stomach twisted and bounced, making me ill inside while my lungs slowed down and made my breathing quick and hasty. I felt moisture in my eyes from the sheer embarrassment that this angelic creation of God had seen the horrid me, but I could not stop. His face was thin, yet healthy, with a lovely head of caramel-colored and curly hair on the top. Lance's arms were extremely thin like mine, but slender and charming as he held his ham and cheese sandwich in his gentle hands. However, the feature I admired most about him were his eyes; gorgeous eyes that were the color of an enchanting forest, shining a light shade of lime green, with mysterious traits hidden within them. This vision in color was a world better than the perfect picture I had memorized.

What was a girl to do? In a state of panic, I grabbed Oliver and began to hug him for comfort. What was wrong with me? All I wanted to do was run and cry in darkness. Lance should not be looking at a stick made of only ugliness when he deserves a fair beauty.

Yet, my fate had been sealed. From out of nowhere, I heard him say in the most innocent and attractive voice, "You are hugging on Oliver so much, why not be his girlfriend?" He sounded hurt, like I had stabbed him in the heart. I was a horrible person, using my friend for support, upsetting a creature so wonderful . . . I had failed as a person.

I turned my head away from the group, apologized as sweetly and calmly as I could and ran out the door. Once up the stairs, I caught my breath and forced back tears of depression. I was not sure why I cared so much, but I could not deny it anymore. I was in love with Lance Conwell and he hated me.

The next hour dragged for me for I had the burden of carrying this heavy weight forever on my tired back. Choir class was difficult, for of all the days, it was the day the girls' and guys' choirs sang together for the Christmas concert and Lance was on the same row as me. All I did was stare at him from the corner of my eye and I blushed so much that my section asked if I was having a heat stroke. I tried to focus on the music, but I failed horribly for all my eyes wanted to see was Lance. For once, I was glad to get out of class to my final hour. As I placed my folder quickly in my slot, I felt a figure approach me from behind. In fright, I jumped and turned to look into the eyes of Lance, whose eyes were huge and deer in the headlights like for I startled him.

"I am so sorry!" I screamed, worried I would upset him more.

He smiled lightly and warmly, making my heart melt and knees go extremely weak. "It is okay." Elegantly, he brushed his hand through his soft hair and stared at the ground for a moment to collect his thoughts. "I just, well, I, hmmm, wanted to say hey and tell you that, ummmm, you sing well . . . yeah! That you sing well," he said with a sweet laugh and shrug.

Lance was not mad at me! I had never been so happy in my life. I got close to his face, scaring him once more and smiled widely. "Thank you so much!" The bell was about to ring, making my flying heart slowly float down. "Lance . . ." I said shyly. "Can I . . . well, hug you?"

In shock, he bent back, almost tripping on his bag with his face candy apple red and his doe eyes huge. He gulped loudly before answering my request. "Sure."

I lightly wrapped my arms around him and hugged him, feeling his warmth. The sensation was incredible; I never wanted to let go of this feeling. I stared quickly into his eyes which were so beautiful and ready to protect. He replied my glance by looking deeply into my eyes with kindness and concern that made me blush again. My perfect moment was not meant to last for eternity, for the warning bell rang loudly, shattering my soul. In slow motion, I let go and told him good-bye, full of compassion and sorrow for I was leaving the side of my crush, no, the guy I loved and was in dire pain every time I had to leave him. To me, Spanish class was shining in a veil of golden glory because *he* hugged me. I could not wait to go home to lie under my warm blue star comforter and relive that magical moment all weekend. I only had one more hour to go.

Twirling on cloud nine and driving my peers to insanity, I was all smiles when school was dismissed for the day. To further my bright mood, I hummed a catchy melody that I learned in choir class named "Glory on High" down the hallway. A bright ray of light reflected off the shining white tile and blinded my sensitive eyes. Suddenly, I spotted Lance sitting on the wooden bench, nervously looking at the same tile I did only seconds before. After swallowing my heart, I took a long, lasting breath and quietly took steps toward him.

"Hey Lance," I managed to choke out after being temporarily frozen by his beauty. "What are you doing here?" This was a sincere question for I have never seen him after school; I would have noticed someone like him!

"Oh, my mom is going to college and has an exam today, so I have to wait for her until four. When does your ride get here?"

"The usual, 3:30. Would you like me to wait with you?"

"Sure, I would really like that." Lance gave me a grand smile and I sat by him as closely as I could without him feeling awkward. Together, we had light conversation and stared at each other lovingly for about twenty minutes. I loved his grace, the sweet way he laughed, the way his hair bounced naturally and how the light beamed off his skin to give it a lovely glow.

All I wanted was for him to like me the way I did him, yet why would a smart guy like me? No matter how kind and sweet he was and even if he hugged me, Lance Conwell would never love me. Each time I gazed at him, it made my heart crumble more for I could never have his heart; nowhere near pretty enough for a prince like him.

From out of the blue, my heart took over my mouth and blurted the phrase I locked inside my soul: "Would you like to go out with me?" In horror, I gasped loudly and painfully covered my mouth with my hand. I jerked my head away from him with tears trying to escape my eyes. Where did this come from? I ruined my chance to have this handsome young man as my friend.

"Sure, I would love to," I heard lightly and kindly. I gasped again with my tears still forming and slowly turned to see his face bright red, but with the warmest grin. In shock, my eyes began to sparkle, yet my face was in a confused daze. He must have felt my vibe. "The truth is, I was planning on asking you out. I know it is crazy of me, but I just cannot help it. Ever since I saw you yesterday and Oliver talked about you . . . I fell for you. I was the one that begged for a picture of you and I was surprised . . . you were a lot cuter than Oliver mentioned and seeing you in the flesh . . . wow! I think you are the most beautiful thing I have ever seen, which is why I was so angry that you were hugging Oliver; I was jealous and wishing it was me."

I could not believe what I was hearing. The one boy I fell for not only liked me, but was nuts about me as I was for him. I have never felt more wonderful in my life. At the exact same moment, we both grabbed each other's hand and laced our figures delicately together, blushing slightly in unison as well. I had never been so happy and to this day, have never felt so important. That fateful day, I had been loved and it decided my destiny. Lance completes me to this very moment and he does anything for me; he is my soul, my spirit, my heart; he is a part of my being. While my friends have gone through boy after boy as fast as the breeze makes leaves fall off the trees in autumn, I have been more than content with Lance. I am no longer a duckling nor have I become a swan. All that matters is that Lance makes me feel like I am beautiful.

Super Short Poems, Journals, and Other Literary Works

"Guys can hurt your emotions, breaking the gate, allowing the flood to wash you away. We, as girls, struggle to stay afloat, but painfully succeed. There, we see the guy being harmed by his own emotions and drowning for the pain he caused."

—Morgan Straughan Comnick

Like the page states, these are super short poems I wrote and then other, random types of literary works I have done. Take a look! All the short poems are from 2006 to 2007.

The following poem was inspired by: Class assignment and the weather on that day

Sleeping Earth

Hands shaking in chill
Hair blowing like wild fire
Body frozen from nipping air
Jack Frost smiling at my utter desire

Breath the shape of smoke
Eyes watering from the sting
This is not how I imagined
The first day of Spring!

Inspired by: Class assignment and penguins, because my friend is scared of them!

Arctic Fun

The earth sparkling in white
The ground mushy and the water cold
The weather is beautiful mixing with our sun
Come friends, let's dance and be bold!

Inspired by: Class assignment

Dedicated to: The St. Louis Cardinals (they were training in Florida while we were having 35 or below weather . . . Lucky them!)

A Bird's Eye View

A gentle breeze hitting the window
Sun blazing on the emerald-colored ground
Working hard to practice my dream
The sign of peace all around

I admit, my heart is lonely
My house, family; love is the key
Yet, I am glad not to be stuck in snow
in my cold, home state of Missouri!

Inspired by: Another boredom poem. I saw a friend smile and I thought I'd try an old school technique

Smile

Sunshine
Magical
Interesting
Loving
Everything

Inspired by: Another boredom poem. I thought of the 2nd *Sailor Moon R* opening where she is swirling with the clocks, listening. It's related to my current mood. I got the title from an *InuYasha* icon I saw.

Between Worlds

Myself is locked in time
Spinning, Listening, Blinking
I act too calm for reality
Too shaken for fantasy
I'm in between two worlds

Inspired by: Mr. Behr's class, where I aided, did a quick poem project where they had to use ten words from a list I used like twenty! HA! It was fun and pieced itself together.

Dedicated to: All who do not realize fear is the absence of faith.

Visions

A ripple forms on the moon
Whisper your enchantment to the midnight
Glare at the fire and icy feelings of hate
A mirror glitters the spiral of doubt
Destroy life's shimmering lighting
Then, your emerald world will dance
Soon, the evil thunderstorm will bubble away
And the photographs of a wedding appear

We had to describe a place of comfort to us at the start of my junior communication arts year (2005). Ah! This was the year I discovered the author Lurlene McDaniel and I was asked by a teacher to stop sending in book reports for bonus points for I had fourteen more books than everyone else! HA! She actually said my reading was causing more work! I still think that's funny, but this was a fun year for me.

My Comfort Zone

The dull, bland walls were covered with rows of unique and colorful posters. The sun lightly shone on the silver screen, reflecting small disks of prisms. A pale, soft chair was piled high with many cushions, gracefully arranged to show their importance. Rich, beautiful colors were set on top of a cream stand, showing how creative the items of Asia are. Stars, a dark sea of stars covered her rest place and sparkled under the moonlight. Adorable stuffed animals and dolls were resting peacefully on soft, lavender pillows. A hidden treasure was behind the door: wonderful books, rows of knowledge. Her friends were hidden in her desk drawer, yet they were very much loved along with her photo albums, CDs, video games, and drawing supplies also tucked there. Everything was in the perfect place.

This is her *comfort* zone, my *comfort* zone. This is *my room.*

All righty! Going back in time a little bit! In sixth grade, I had a grand language teacher named Mrs. Horton and she was the one who first dubbed me "The Queen of Details." Since then, I worked hard to keep up that type of writing style I enjoy so much. Since she was also my history teacher, we had to do journals on Ellis Island and here is what I wrote. I went through several edits as a kid, but I made this as smooth as possible. I wrote this in 2001.

4, March 1908

Dear Diary,

Today, me and my family left for Ellis Island. My family is Papa, Mama, Jake (age 20), Mickeal (age 24), Lisa (age 19), Nickolas (age 8), Breanna, (age 7), Alex, Colton, and Josh (all age 4), and of course, there is me, Chyna (China) E. Hutchings. I do think I have a big family. My grandparents left to Ellis Island last March. All I have is my clothes, a few pieces of rolls, a necklace, my rag doll Megan, and 30 cents. I was so scared of what would happen when I got on the ship. I am only 11, but I will be 12 on May first. I hope we are on the island soon and my family will be fine.

25, March 1908

Breanna and I raced to the deck to look at the sea. Today was a pretty day to run, but one of the workers yelled at us to stop. We did. We went to our bed to play with our dolls, Rebecca and Megan. Before I prayed for the sick, Lisa came in and told us she would play with us! I could hear seagulls and the waves against the ship while we played. Jake came in and told us a storm was coming. I am now scared because Alex, Colton, and Nick kept crying while Breanna hid. Mama got sick, Lisa worried, and Jake and Mickeal told stories of people who were killed in storms. They got so bad that other people in our cabin ran away.

Papa is the only one I can trust. He is brave yet he keeps us as safe as he can. I always go by Papa in a storm. I could smell the salt in the air afterwards. The night became warm and lovely. I fell asleep looking at the moon and stars in the dark sky.

27, March 1908

Mama is going to have a baby! The doctors in France (my old country) thought the baby had died, but the sick doctors have found a heartbeat, a fine one! I love babies! That's the good news, the bad news is Colton is ill. I am working hard to keep him well. Everyone is, even a sailor came to help him. He was bringing soup to help Colton's voice. I never have felt happy and sad before. I see the sky is feeling my pain because half of it is sunny and half is cloudy. I smell my tears of joy for Mama and my tears of sorrow for Colton. I hope everything will be alright.

28, March 1908

Colton is better! He only has trouble walking now! Mama is taking one of my old dresses to give to the baby since I won't need it. I met a girl named Natalia. She's from Russia and very nice. I don't understand her, but we both move our hands when we talk. We are very silly together! When I'm around her, I forget my troubles of being a child. I told her about a flood that killed many animals and crops in my area. People were so desperate that they came and took a lot of money. Later, a huge fire hit our town and burned all the houses, including ours. She told me of the tsar, her brothers Jon and Jim, and how her mom died on the ship and now, her dad is sick. I told her good-bye on the second floor (she is on it with me too). Breanna, Lisa, Mama, and I ran to see the sunset on the water. It was beautiful, like a painting. I smelled Mama's sweet hands. They smelled like roses. I felt sparkling with hope like the sea, yet my bright dreams went down like the sun.

30, April 1908

Today, the baby was born! It is so beautiful! It is a boy named Allen. Natalia waited with me outside the room. A sailor came in with a small pail of water for Mama. Papa came out about an hour later with a big smile and said, "It's a boy." Natalia, Breanna, and I yelled happily, jumping up and down and danced together. I ran in and saw Allen. He kicked his legs up like my old horse. I kissed his head and hugged my Megan doll close. I smelled the baby's sweet, oily head and smiled with happiness.

01, May 1908

I am now twelve and so happy because today, we got to Ellis Island! Everyone cried, even Jake. Mama said that she did not buy me a birthday gift, but I said, "Getting here is the best gift I ever got!" I saw children reading, writing, and playing, like I would someday. All these people are acting very strange to me because they are checking my eyes and other things. I cannot wait until my family and I are happy in America. People gave me food and a place on the floor to sleep. I am dizzy from the ship. Today was the greatest birthday!

02, May 1908

Today, I met a few other children. Li, Madison, Carda, and Alan, who laughs a lot. They are from Britain. We all played together. They have been here on Ellis Island for two months, still waiting for clearing. I hope we do not end up like that.

20, May 1933

I was trying to find my old lamp my mama gave me and I found a picture of my family and one of us on Ellis Island. I am now starting a journal because my old one burned in the fire of 1920. I hate that fire a lot because Josh got sick from breathing in the ashes. The doctor said he would die. He still is alive, but cannot walk anymore. I am married to a man named Li Syaoron from Britain. I met him outside of Ellis Island after we got accepted into America. I showed the picture of my family I found to my kids. Their names are Melody and Eric. They are wonderful! Their smiles made me think of my grandfather. He died in 1917 and Grandma, who died last year. Their laughs remind me of my friend Alan. He was my neighbor once we moved in to our new home. He died in 1910, not yet fifteen. Seeing this death opened my eyes to the world.

But, I am blessed. I have a lot of money and our friends live close by. Breanna and her husband and Colton and Alex do too. Mama and Papa visit us often. Nick and his wife, Mandy, come every three months. They get to travel all over the place. I only see Jake and Lisa twice a year for holidays. Mickeal? You never know! I am thirty-eight and a teacher now. I love it! I know my thirteen year Eric and ten year old Melody cannot wait for me to show them more.

Chyna Hutchings Syaoron

We also did a unit (I think before Ellis Island, which would make sense) on the Middle Ages. This was the year I got into the Middle Ages, Ancient Greece and Egypt, along with learning about different religions! Funnily . . . I have a summer school class on most of these topics . . . Hmmm . . .

I worked so hard on this journal on my kitchen counter! We tore up an old brown washcloth and laced my fringed pages through it with white ribbon! I even added something at the end to put it over the top (described at the end). My teacher gave me an A+! ☺ So, let's see the life of a medieval serf, shall we? I would have been eleven when I wrote this, in the sixth grade.

01, January 1525

I am thinking of Father and a new year. I hope Lord William will be giving us more rights. Cleaning, cooking, and going to the well is not the best life. I would love to be free! My father died when I was three years old. I really miss him. I was an only child and I still am. I was born in my house, part of the Lord William's castle and land. It was on November 1, 1515 in Bradfort, England. My mother got sick, but luckily got through it and is fine now. I was born healthy and full of life. My mom says I am the joy of her life and I love her very much. I wish I could have seen me be born. I am glad the Lord is nice on my birthday. I cannot wait to be ten! I hope this new year is better than the last ones!

Morgana E. Straughan

19, January 1525

I have heard news from Father Barton. He said that Martin Luther, a monk, married a 'former' nun, Katherine Von Bora. They ran away to start a new way for churches everywhere! The week after this, I heard from Father Barton that England has signed a peace treaty with France. News is coming everywhere. What is next?

Morgana E. Straughan

01, May 1525

Winnie

About a month ago, I found a small, little dog, hurt, and tired, lying on the ground with big, sad eyes. I ran to my little hay bed and put it down to rest. Father Barton would be coming soon to help. He came and told me to find seven plants and herbs, plus four kinds of berries in the morning and he gave me drawings of what they looked like. I ran to the well and boiled the water to heal the cuts of the dog. I dried it with sheep's wool and tied yak hair slowly, and a bit loosely, around it to help. The dog went to sleep by the hay with a little smile of joy and pride.

I wrapped a small, old cloth over her to help keep her warm. Mother came in, but luckily, did not see the dog. Mother cooked me bread and a little piece of ham. Mother left a while ago. I gave some of my ham to the dog. It loved it. Then, the dog went back to sleep. When I woke up, Mother had been to the castle already. Father Barton told me the dog was a girl. I named her Winnie. She is a Yorkshire terrier from Scotland.

Father Barton said her old owner maybe worked at a shop for some money for their families. The owner came a few weeks later. His name is Sir Martin. He wanted "Clara" back from me. But, Winnie did not want to go with him. Father finally gave me two franks to buy Winnie, but Sir Martin wanted five! That is a lot of franks, but I gave him half franks and made him some wool. I got to keep Winnie, but I was worried. I loved Winnie a lot, but when should I tell Mother? What if Lord William finds out? And what if Sir Martin tries to steal her?

Mom now knows and so far, no one has bothered Winnie yet. Father Barton is keeping my secret. Winnie is one of my best friends ever and we are very happy together!
Morgana E. Straughan

27th, June 1526
Father Barton

Father Barton and I have known each other for two years today. I remember when we met. I was helping Mother clean the castle floors when I bumped in to him. He helped me up and after that, we became very fast, very good friends. Every night now, after sunset, he gives Winnie and I a piece of pepper meat. It is so good!

Secretly, he gave me writing lessons and teaches me how to pray right and talk to God and Father. On my birthday, he gave me a beautiful little cross to wear under my clothes. He helps me with my chores from time to time and stands up for the serfs. Recently, he has been teaching me how to read signs and little words. He told me he might have to go back to the town of Bath, but luckily, he stayed for now. He does have a great job here. He decided two days ago to take a quick trip to visit his family. I miss him.

Morgana E. Straughan

14, February 1531

Today, I saw a young boy named Nickolas the III, a squire at age seventeen he was. He came for a few weeks for Lord McBride. He was watching the serfs in the gardens of Lord William. He came over and helped me with the water I was carrying to the Lord. He was very nice and very, very cute!

He helped me and then said he had to go back to Lord McBride's castle to win his knighthood. But that he would stay for my birthday. He gave me the most beautiful necklace in the world! He asked Lord McBride and Lord William if he could marry me. They said no and forced him to leave . . .

Morgana E. Straughan

01, November 1531

Mother has died on my sixteenth birthday today . . . What do I have left since Nickolas, who was allowed to visit, had to leave after our funeral service? I miss you Mother! I am glad you are now with Father, your love. I hope mine, Nickolas, will return.

Morgana E. Straughan

29, December 1532

Today, I got in trouble. I went to the Cathedral to talk to God, Father, and Mother and pray for the safety of Nicholas. I got caught. I got more chores from Lord William as punishment. I stay and sleep with Father Barton now. I want to be with Mother and Father, but stay on Earth too. I plan to run away tonight with Winnie!

I got everything I need to go.

Morgana E. Straughan

Early Morning on 30, December 1532

Winnie and I ran hurriedly, but they saw me! The guards. Winnie and I ran so fast that I almost lost all my supplies. I fell in a big hole. I cannot stand up. I cannot get out. Winnie landed above the hole and I told her to run to get Father Barton. She has not come back yet.

I feel sick and I am bleeding all over. All I have in the hole with me is my journal and my precious ink and quill, gifts from Father Barton for my last birthday.

My will is dying, that means I will die soon. I will finally be free, free in Heaven. Good-bye world . . .

Morgana E. Straughan

I put fake blood at the bottom of the page and rubbed a black ink pen over it to make it look dried! I sure was a dedicated student!

"Just your basic, average girl. (=
♡ Morgan

We had to write a table of contents about our lives at the end of our junior year (2006). Everyone liked mine and a few people asked if I'd write theirs. Geez! Still, it makes my life *sound* more exciting than it probably really was!

When the Stars Lead the Way

A story about the life of Morgan Straughan

Table of Contents:

Chapter 1: One that lives in the seas (birth to age 2)
Chapter 2: When the watchful eyes are closed (age 2-3)
Chapter 3: Skipping in sunshine with him (ages 3-4)
Chapter 4: A brother and a million headaches (ages 5-6)
Chapter 5: A new side of Grandpa (age 7)
Chapter 6: A new experience named love (ages 8-9)
Chapter 7: My dearest role model, my friend (ages 10-11)
Chapter 8: Changing more than classes (age 11)
Chapter 9: Moving on up! Not letting go! (age 12)
Chapter 10: Shall we dance? (age 12)
Chapter 11: The year guys "wanted me" (ages 12-13)
Chapter 12: Connecting to Britain (ages 13-14)
Chapter 13: True test of friendship (age 14)
Chapter 14: Dad's new role (age 14)
Chapter 15: A novelist is sparked (ages 14-15)
Chapter 16: Watching a legend say farewell (age 15)
Epilogue: What's next? (current)

Thanks

"I need a friend who understands and accepts that I know all my cars from *Twilight*, my hair is long because I idolize *Sailor Moon*, I'm secretly a Power Ranger, and that 'I want to be the very best, like no one ever was.'"

—Morgan Straughan Comnick

I have so many wonderful people to thank!

I want to thank my mom for giving me my creative spirit and support in the arts.

I want to thank my dad for instilling in me how hard work pays off and how to analyze the world in the right way.

My brothers, Miles and Jon, for knowing the true, goofy me better than anyone.

My darling, my husband, Derrick, for making love so easy to write about; he is the perfect muse.

My friends and Farmington high classmates, especially Marissa, Kristen, and Erin, who went through all these high school adventures with me and through thick and thin, we survived, grew, and have great memories.

My school, for being the doors that started a journey in writing I never could have imagined or created on my own.

My hometown for being the perfect landscape, inside and out, for all these words.

My language arts teachers for pushing me, giving me knowledge, and driving me crazy! Any teacher who had me, too! Thanks for being my stepping stones to life!

My Lord, my God, for giving me all these blessings. I make sure to count them daily.

For Paper Crane Books and my publisher Sheenah for allowing my younger self to make an appearance. My younger self is very grateful and hopes she is liked.

Everyone who knows me now, for your continual support and words and gestures of kindness. No matter if we met from random encounters, anime conventions, work, church, other people, life, or so forth, I hope the younger me does not scare you off too much!

And, last, but not least, to you loyal readers and fans, for making me push myself to new heights because you believe in me. What will you have me doing next?

See you next time!

Love always,
Morgan Straughan Comnick

Music had always soothed my soul since I got chosen for choir in sixth grade. High school choir changed my life in so many wonderful ways. I grew more confident, got to sing my heart out, meet new friends, have lasting memories, and I met Derrick through choir as well. Our director, Sue Bauche, is what made this choir for me, for all of us, so special. You could not ask for a woman who would do anything for you more, who would make you laugh and love to come to school every day.

She passed away after a hard fight with cancer fall of 2013. I still cannot imagine a world without her love and music. She made us all feel special, writing to us in our journals, giving us advice even if we didn't want to hear it, and or squeezing us in a bear hug so massive that you thought your lungs would burst, but you loved it. She was our home, our safe haven, our reasons to grow. Everyone who told stories about her have said similar things. I was never the best at anything kind or most noticeable, but she still loved me, was there for me, trusted me . . . even now.

Right before I got the edits for this collection, I was having a very rough evening, life overwhelming me with all I had to do. I curled up on my couch, listening to the deafening noises of our wall clock, every little sound hurting my racing mind more. I usually do not ask for help from others, but I curled deeper into the couch and asked for someone to please help me figure all this out. After this, her name passed through my lips. A few seconds later, I felt a firm, but loving touch on my right shoulder, and a phrase as clear as day, as clear as I would have heard it in class years ago, "Oh . . . baby . . ." I bolted upright and looked everywhere, seeing her smiling face with gold around it in my head. It was there for a second, only a second, her hardy laugh engulfing me as her tone still had its "let me tell you how it is" attitude. I had never felt or heard anything so real in so, so long, but I was alone in my living room. And, with her touch and words, I cried and cried. I cried myself to sleep, something I have never done. I woke up two hours later and stumbled into bed, the echoes of her words still ringing in my head, her touch still grabbing at my heart. I slept well for eight hours thinking of her. I woke up, feeling still nervous, but ready to face all the challenges ahead of me. Nothing was solved, but knowing she still was taking care of me all this time, recalling all the hardship she had to face and still, she managed to crawl to school because of her love for us and her music, cleared my doubts.

So, to all my fellow Bauche babies, Mrs. Bauche is still watching out for us. You may not believe my story, but I promise you, she was with me that night, helping me jump over this hurdle. Mrs. Bauche, you always called us your angels . . . now you are our guardian angel. Thank you from the bottom of my heart for all the love, music, and belief.

I dedicate this collection of mine to Mrs. Sue Bauche and everyone she has touched.

Morgan Straughan Comnick (Choir: 2003-2007)

About the Author

Educator of young minds by day, super nerdy savior of justice and cute things by night, Morgan Straughan Comnick has a love for turning the normal into something special without losing its essence. Morgan draws from real life experiences and her ongoing imagination to spark her writing. In her spare time, she enjoys doing goofy voices, traveling to new worlds by turning pages, humming child-like songs, and forcing people to smile with her "bubbliness." It is Morgan's mission in life to spread the amazement of otaku/Japanese culture to the world and to stop bullying; she knows everyone shines brightly.

To learn more, visit her at her website: morganscomnick.com